What People Are Saying About
God, a Motorcycle, and the Open Road

"Tim Riter has written a fun and th[...]
lessons he's learned from the open [...]
from an open Bible. I encourage y[...]
you can learn."

Larry Osborne, pastor and author
North Coast Church, Vista, California

"Tim has uniquely combined God's Word with motorcycling in such a fashion that one can understand just what it means to be more like the Father. Hit this book each day before your ride and watch what God does in your life."

Frank Pomeroy, pastor, First Baptist Church, Sutherland Springs
(on two wheels almost 40 years, riding an Ultra-Glide)

"Even nonbikers like myself are in for a treat as we hit the open road with Tim, his bike, and God. A great read!"

Nick Harrison, author of *One-Minute Prayers® for Husbands*
and *One-Minute Prayers® for Dads*

"I could almost feel the wind in my face. The insights Tim shares from countless experiences will make you more sensitive to the prompting of the Holy Spirit."

John Derry, PhD, president of Hope
International University, Fullerton

"A WINNER! Tim can write, and he has an eye for beauty and color and people and landscapes. He also has a soul bent on freedom in Christ, and the ride and the road are really metaphors for the kind of freedom he believes God wants everyone to enjoy. I can't recommend this book highly enough. And Tim is not just talking to the church here. This book is for anyone aching for a real God and a real life."

Murray Pura, author of *Majestic and Wild, A Road Called Love,*
and *The Wings of Morning*

"Tim Riter does a good job encouraging bikers to put wheels to their faith. Or vice versa."

Andy Cripe, member, Christian Motorcyclists Association

"*God, a Motorcycle, and the Open Road* is filled with provocative, compelling, and heartfelt insights gleaned on the back of a bike. Whether it's a Harley or a Honda, saddle up for the trip with Tim Riter as your ride leader."

Steve Redden, pastor, Crosspoint Church, Temecula

"Who knew so many analogies to our walk with God could come from riding motorcycles with great friends? I'm so glad I got to be a part of the experience."

Jerry Christensen, pastor, Honda Gold Wing
and more, rider for 50 years

"Tim inspires me to be a better person. To be a better rider. To be more faithful to Christ. I trust this book will inspire you."

Greg England, Suzuki Boulevard, 65 years old, 18 months a biker

"Tim has a down-to-earth writing style that flows smoothly from his motorcycle experiences to the spiritual lessons he has learned."

Dan DeWitt, pastor for 33 years and biker for 46 years

"Tim offers a new perspective—to view life in terms of the journey God is unfolding, connecting us to the beauty of both the Creator and His creation. It focuses on life as an act of worship."

Les Enloe, author and screenwriter

GOD,
A MOTORCYCLE,
AND THE
OPEN ROAD

TIM RITER

HARVEST HOUSE PUBLISHERS
EUGENE, OREGON

Cover by Bryce Williamson

Cover photos © Man_Half-tube, studiogstock, oriontrail / Getty

Author photo © by Joshua D. Garcia

Published in association with the literary agency of WordServe Literary Group, Ltd., www.word serveliterary.com.

Italics in quoted Scriptures indicate emphasis added by the author.

God, a Motorcycle, and the Open Road
Copyright © 2019 by Tim Riter
Published by Harvest House Publishers
Eugene, Oregon 97408
www.harvesthousepublishers.com

ISBN 978-0-7369-7550-6 (pbk.)
ISBN 978-0-7369-7551-3 (eBook)

Library of Congress Cataloging-in-Publication Data

Names: Riter, Tim, author.
Title: God, a motorcycle, and the open road / Tim Riter.
Description: Eugene : Harvest House Publishers, 2019.
Identifiers: LCCN 2018049549 (print) | LCCN 2019000865 (ebook) | ISBN 9780736975513 (ebook) | ISBN 9780736975506 (pbk.)
Subjects: LCSH: Christian life. | Riter, Tim, 1948---Travel. | Motorcycling.
Classification: LCC BV4501.3 (ebook) | LCC BV4501.3 .R578 2019 (print) | DDC 277.3/083082 [B] --dc23
LC record available at https://lccn.loc.gov/2018049549

Printed in the United States of America

19 20 21 22 23 24 25 26 27 / VP-GL / 10 9 8 7 6 5 4 3 2 1

God, a Motorcycle, and the Open Road is dedicated
to all the riders who led the way, who taught me
to thrive and survive on two wheels.

My dad, Lynn Riter, resides at the top of that list. He first
delivered telegrams in Los Angeles on a belt-drive Excelsior bike, later an Indian, and set a world record in the
Cannonball cross-country run in a Ford Model A. I suspect he passed on to me the drive to challenge myself.

The Gray Hogs—our regular riding crew of Jerry, Rich,
Mick, and Brad—have shared a lot of miles and smiles
over a lot of years. Thanks for the rich rides, my friends.
Larry Clark built my second bike, a semichopped custom
'73 Honda CB 750; I still remember his tips.

And my wife, Sheila, who took a lot of rides, including
some long ones. In one hot desert stretch, she mopped my
head and neck with cool water to keep us alive.
And though she can't ride now, she graciously supports
my continued insanity of riding.

Most of all, to God, who has gifted us with not only grace
but with a beautiful creation, one with enough order
that motorcycles can be designed!

ACKNOWLEDGMENTS

Getting a book out takes a lot of work from a lot of people. So, great thanks to my agent Sarah Freese of WordServe Literary, who not only got my writing and goals, but also got Todd Hafer at Harvest House to take a look at a bit of an unusual book. *Muchas gracias*, Todd. More thanks to Kim Moore and the entire Mackenzie Team, who shepherded the book through 15 different readings, and to the other editors and production people and sales and marketing, who all caught the vision of reaching people through biker stories!

And acknowledgments would remain incomplete without appreciation to Bryce Williamson, who led his team to a perfect cover for a biker book. And yes, the style of the logo was intentional. Hope you got that blending of the logos of two major bike brands.

I pray that all of your work will result in many lives beginning to see how God touches every part of life, not just motorcycling.

CONTENTS

FOREWORD

More than four decades ago I read *Zen and the Art of Motorcycle Maintenance*, Robert Pirsig's personal narrative on metaphysics and the lessons possible while journeying across America on two wheels. Drawing on both his knowledge of the mechanics of a motorcycle and Plato's dialogues, Pirsig shared his search for answers to big questions few truly confront over the course of a lifetime.

Like Robert Pirsig, my friend Tim Riter has gifted us with a saga of lessons to be learned from the seat of a motorcycle. Unlike Pirsig, however, Tim draws on the 240,000 miles he has ridden across North America to reveal the connection between his love of "the ride" and his deep faith in Christianity.

Tim's narrative is both personal and accessible. He shares how the experience of riding a motorcycle has served to both inform and enrich his personal relationship with Christ. If the reader's faith is broadened or made richer in the process, I think Tim would simply smile with contentment.

That said, Tim's narrative is not neutral. The sacred text on which his faith is founded is liberally shared and connected with anecdotes drawn from the people and places he's experienced from the iron butt throne.

This is also a book of themes. My favorites struck me as universal in their truths. They include, but are not limited to, our need for:

- love, unity, and harmony in our lives
- forgiveness

- civility and respect offered to others
- humility
- openness
- overcoming unjustified fear
- balance in our lives

In other words, themes Christ and his disciples returned to again and again.

Tim's love for the undeniable beauty God created in the physical world also deserves mention. Traveling across the landscape on two wheels, as anyone who has ridden knows firsthand, means making yourself vulnerable to not just risk but to the fact that with dominion comes enormous responsibility.

I hope the preceding convinces you that even though Tim wears his faith on the sleeve of his leathers, his narrative is well suited to anyone in search of a spiritual connection to something larger than themselves. Enjoy, and please discuss what Tim shares. If you can do it with a sore butt and bugs in your teeth after a long ride, then all the better.

Mike Scott,

lifelong rider of open roads and lover of the adventure inherent in two wheels

1

GETTING INTO IT

The Miracle of a Motorcycle

Ride majestically!
Ride triumphantly!
Ride on the side of truth!
Ride for the righteous meek!

PSALM 45:3-4 MSG

Bikes captivate us. The fears that we face and still ride. The companionships we develop. The fresh country we'd never experience except for them. The clichéd but true freedom of the open road. The immersion in God's world, unprotected by a cage of steel and glass. The changes they lead us to. The time to ponder God and our lives and to see his glory and how we can bring him more.

But for years bikes held no interest for me. Never desired to hop on one. Until, in the summer before my senior year in college, a neighbor almost forced me to try his kids' Honda Trail 90. Just to shut him up, I did. Nice. Not captivating. But nice.

Then, near the end of my senior year, my college roommate and I planned on taking my 1964 Ford Falcon to Canada to visit a friend who had moved there. Then Murphy stepped in. Mark didn't have the money, and a lady ran into my Falcon on a Los Angeles freeway.

I didn't feel confident driving it that far, and the trip began to look pretty shaky.

But during my final finals week, several of us got tired of studying and headed for a local theater to see *Easy Rider*, the iconic cult film depicting sex, drugs, and bikes. I was entranced. Not with the sex and drugs, although I certainly wasn't walking with Jesus then. But Peter Fonda and Dennis Hopper captured the freedom of traveling on two wheels out in nature, which captivated me.

Then the idea burst upon me like inspiration—work for a few months, save enough to buy a bike, and head to Canada for a month before grad school started.

A life-changing event. I bought a new 1970 Honda 350 Scrambler, a cross between a road bike and a dirt bike. Much too small for such a trip. Much too multipurpose for a long tour. Three weeks after the purchase, I took off. Much too soon for a rookie rider. I did make it back for the start of grad school, but more importantly, I graduated into motorcycling. I discovered how a motorcycle could lead to a miracle of a new life.

That first ride on the little Honda 90 pleased me, *Easy Rider* intrigued me, but my first motorcycle tour transformed me.

Since then I've driven more than 240,000 miles on two wheels. I really can't count the number of multistate trips, but it's in the dozens. One alone covered 31 states and 13,000 miles. As I can best figure, so far I've only missed four states while on two wheels. I've changed a flat tire in 110-degree heat and unjammed a chain that slipped off the sprocket and locked the rear wheel on the side of a Canadian mountain road. Returning from a ride to Colorado, I had a main fuse blow and stall my bike on a downtown Los Angeles freeway during rush hour. I eased my way to the side, fixed it, and rode on.

I have grease under my fingernails and a lot of miles on my butt.

Just last summer, I completed my second Iron Butt run—1,080 miles on two wheels within 24 hours—from my home in Temecula to Dillon, Montana.

I know a bit about riding and have learned the close connection with faith that riding has for me and a lot of others. Faith that my tires will hold their grip on a wet road. Faith the room I reserved for the end of a rainy day will be there. Faith that my riding buddies will make the trip better, not worse. Mostly, I've seen how motorcycling has enriched my faith in God and how faith has enriched my motorcycling.

I began following Jesus at age 11, until the shallowness of my faith led to four years of questioning and searching in college. Ironically, that first Canada trip played a key role in coming back to God. I've been with him ever since. I've pastored churches and written books about living as a follower of Jesus.

So, this book. A collection of stories and thoughts and meditations and questions about the intersection of these two passions. Devotions? Yes, but hopefully a bit more. Not so much affirming as challenging. A challenge to blend these in your life as well. Hard-won truths, iron-butt hard. Some questions that may cause you to think of riding or Christianity in a new light.

Use them as best fits you. If you're in a group, maybe read one chapter at a meeting and kick it around a bit. Or, on a ride, start the day with one. Give the book away to fellow riders that may not yet know Jesus. This isn't an evangelistic tract, but it might help them see Jesus in a fresh way.

And let me know if this book works for you. If it sells enough, we can do more. I'd love the next book to focus on the experiences others have found while easy riding. So if you have a story or two to tell, send me an email at timriter@aol.com to find out how to do that.

KICK-STARTING THE APPLICATION

Do you ride now? What first attracted you? Think back to the bikes you've had, the good experiences and the bad. How has riding impacted your faith? Would you like to build a closer connection to riding and following Jesus? If you don't ride, have you ever thought of a spiritual link between faith and riding?

2

★ TWO-WHEELED UNITY

Why Can't We All Just Get Along?

The dangers of the Black Hills exceed free-ranging buffalo. Various temptations afflict me, and a sign before a curve commanding me to slow to 35 proved too much. I downshifted my Kawasaki Vulcan and goosed the throttle a bit as I leaned in at about 60, reveling in the bike's responsiveness.

While I balanced the sharpness of the curve, my speed, and the proper lean angle, another bike came toward me, with his left hand held out and down low in the biker's wave. Some hold their whole hand out, others a forefinger, others the first two in a new version of the old peace sign. But on the open road, most do something.

Returning it would slightly change the center of gravity of my bike, adding a level of risk. Not returning it would violate the biker's code. So I waved. Carefully. With some adjustments. But I waved.

Bikers vary. A lot. Some love just one model; others ride anything on two wheels. Some have done it for decades, while weekend riders cruise to a local doughnut shop on Saturday mornings. And we find every step in between.

But we're all bikers, united by a love of wind in our faces, the lure of speed, an appreciation to be in the middle of nature, not insulated in a steel cocoon. A unity that transcends the significant differences many of us have.

How does the metaphor of biker unity apply to followers of Jesus?

The Type of Bike — what do you ride?

I tend to grade other believers on what they ride—their denomination or style of church or their doctrine. If they don't match me, I wonder about them and resist close connections. Now, we have some genuine and significant differences in the Christian family, but if we allow them to interfere with unity, then we miss what it means to follow. If we share Jesus, we need to have a visible unity. Regardless of differences.

How Often They Ride

I also pigeonhole them by how often they ride—regularly or cross-country trips or just those Saturday doughnut shop runs. Do they seem as committed as I prefer to think I am? Are they Christmas/Easter attenders or monthlies or weeklies?

That often encourages us to look down on fellow followers; we view them as less mature, less motivated. But it damages unity.

Keeping It Clean

And don't we sometimes look at them a bit askance if they don't keep their bike as clean as we keep ours? Jerry meticulously cleans his bike every day on our two-week rides. Mick just wipes the bugs off his windshield, and when the trip ends he puts it in the garage and doesn't touch it for a month or two. Each thinks the other might be a bit off.

And we followers often look down on those who don't keep their lives quite as clean. Or whose sins aren't the ones we do. I don't mean to imply that we ignore sins in each other, Galatians 6:1 tells us to deal with them. But do we judge or restore them? The former hurts unity; the latter builds it.

The Lone Wolf

True confession time: I struggle with a tendency to be a lone wolf with both relationships and bikes. I work on both areas and have found going together provides benefits that solo rides can't match. Mick and Brad fixed a key that broke in my gas cap lock or I'd have been stuck.

Sometimes we do the solo spiritual life and have very few connections with others. Maybe we've been burned. Maybe we like anonymity. But either way, we and the church lose the connection with others on the journey that God says we need. So how do we deal with these issues?

Let's go beyond the bike story to see the importance of connecting.

Connecting Is Normative

Last words bear a lot of importance, so look at Jesus' prayer: "I pray also for those who will believe in me through their message, that all of them may be one, Father, just as you are in me and I am in you. May they also be in us so that the world may believe that you have sent me" (John 17:20-21).

All of us. Ducatis and Harleys and Hondas and even Vespas. Visible unity.

Community Is Critical

Okay, God desires unity for his people. But notice the degree of importance.

> Whoever claims to love God yet hates a brother or sister is a liar. For whoever does not love their brother and sister, whom they have seen, cannot love God, whom they have not seen. And he has given us this command: Anyone who loves God must also love their brother and sister (1 John 4:20-21).

Connections Must Be Observable

This one scares me: "By this everyone will know that you are my disciples, if you love one another" (John 13:35). Theologian Francis Schaeffer said the world has the right to say we don't truly believe in Jesus unless they see connection, care, and change in us. Unity. Journeying together. It doesn't get easier, does it?

KICK-STARTING THE APPLICATION

Frankly, we must decide to disagree agreeably. We don't have to agree on all issues; the early church didn't. Study Romans 14 and 15 that explore the principle "As for the man who is weak in faith, welcome him, but not for disputes over opinions" (14:1 RSV). Value our connections more than being right or getting others to agree with us. Discuss the differences, acknowledge them, and we can all learn from one another.

Overall, which attitudes do you have that work against unity with others? What have you done to enhance it? What can you do this week to build more unity? What will be your "wave" to a fellow follower?

DAVID WATSON on CONNECTION

3

FEARING MEN, FEARING GOD

Dealing with Both

The year? 1974. The era? The Watergate frenzy peaked as people wondered if the Nixon presidency could survive the flood of revelations about the break-in and the following cover-up. Earlier in the day I finagled a private after-hours tour of the Rhode Island state capitol to see its charter. The Ocean State was the first American colony to have full religious liberty, and its charter was signed by the king of England himself.

As I looked at the charter in a back room, the nearby telex chattered: Nixon had just scheduled a major address for that evening, had called Vice President Gerald Ford back to DC, and would reportedly resign. I grew up in California, also Nixon's turf, and had to view this. My options were a pricey motel room or a bar. I chose the latter for the price of a beer.

Later that evening I rode the Honda 750 into Groton, Connecticut, not long before the speech, and spotted The Grotto, a long, low bar. One with a television. Free. A wall separated the dimly lit bar from the entry hall, so I turned right and peered inside. Kind of a redneck crowd, where a long-haired hippie biker might not be welcome.

So I turned back into the hallway as another guy did at the

opposite end. Not wanting to cause trouble, I stepped to my left. He stepped to his right. Coincidence. Again I moved to get out of his way and he again moved in front of me. You can guess my thoughts. I repeated my evasive maneuver while trying to not challenge him by looking directly at his eyes. He responded, and my fear grew. Figuring I better make peace before getting pounded, I raised my hands palm up and said, "I don't want any trouble."

This guy also raised his hands and mouthed something. What I thought was a long, open hall had a mirror just past the entry door, and I had scared myself half to death with my own reflection.

Fear. Real or exaggerated or imagined. Here this story takes an unexpected turn. In life, we face many sources of fear, such as scaring myself. All of us who ride need a healthy fear of our bikes and the cost of a crash. But what might be the greatest source of fear? Let me suggest God.

We often diminish the concept of fearing God by calling it reverence or awe. Yes, those fit. But the word for reverence or awe means fear. If we're in Christ, we have no fear regarding punishment. I recall dating a gorgeous girl back in college, one far above me on the status ladder. When I asked her out and she said yes, I almost asked why. She so amazed me I could hardly speak for fear of showing what an idiot I was. Multiply that by a billion or so to get a clue of how much God transcends us.

What are the typical first words of an angel when appearing to a human? "Fear not." Why? Angels have a presence that intimidates humans so much we need that encouragement to not fear. Now, how do the angels view God? "I saw the Lord, high and exalted, seated on a throne; and the train of his robe filled the temple. Above him were seraphim [angels], each with six wings: With two wings they covered their faces, with two they covered their feet, and with two they were flying" (Isaiah 6:1-2). Apparently, the angels covered their faces to avoid seeing God fully and also covered their feet, contaminated by contact with earth. We can't look at angels, and angels can't look at God.

Using the search feature of my Online Bible, 278 passages came up with the words "fear" and "God" or "Lord." Half dealt with fearing life situations or people and relying on God. But the other half talk about fearing God. Fearing God is a huge biblical concept. And the word in the New Testament is the Greek *phobos*, meaning "fear." Take a look at just a few that cover the breadth of the Bible.

"Moses said to the people, 'Do not be afraid. God has come to test you, so that *the fear of God will be with you to keep you from sinning*'" (Exodus 20:20).

"The *fear of the* LORD is the beginning of wisdom" (Proverbs 9:10).

"Show proper respect to everyone, love the family of believers, *fear God*, honor the emperor" (1 Peter 2:17).

"Be subject to one another in the *fear of Christ*" (Ephesians 5:21 NASB).

Why should we fear him? One reason for today: fear combats self-centeredness. We look at our technology, our progress, our achievements, and pride fills us. We're important. Until we see God, and we shrink to near nothingness. Until God's love draws us back to him. Then, and only then, do we possess the balance we need.

Real reasons for humility, as we compare ourselves to God. Real reasons for confidence, as we see our importance to him.

One more reason, from the Exodus passage, given in the same chapter as the Ten Commandments. Being aware of the awesomeness of God, his transcendence, his majesty, serves as an antidote to choosing sin. We don't take God lightly. We don't take disobedience lightly.

Not often do we fear ourselves, like I did. But we ought to fear God, as the angels do. Ironically, that leads to greater intimacy and depth with him. I kinda like that.

KICK-STARTING THE APPLICATION

Do you have any fear of God in regard to his transcendence? Do you think you should have more or less? Why? What are some aspects of God that lead you to a healthy fear of God? How much do you battle self-centeredness? Do you think fear would counter that? For the next few days, ponder the role fear has in getting closer to Jesus.

4

RISKY BUSINESS

The Cost of Hospitality

I can't recall their names, and their faces have faded in memory over time. They gave no hints if they followed Jesus or not. But their actions changed how I live. To set the stage, the resignation of Nixon the day before mostly resolved the Watergate controversy, right in the middle of my bike trip to discover America and a bit of myself. A drizzly day chilled me, so I found a Howard Johnson's a bit north of Boston for some clam chowder.

This hippie biker, with shoulder-length hair and a beard uncut for several months, pulled his semichopped Honda 750 with an *Easy Rider* paint scheme into a parking spot as a family with a dad and mom and five-year-old boy pulled alongside in a sedan. They struck up a conversation, intrigued by a trip with no particular destination, just a desire to see America, so they asked me to join them inside.

"Where do you stay at night?" prompted my response of throwing a sleeping bag down in a rest area or campground.

The dad quickly turned to his wife with a question before turning back to me. "It looks like more rain tonight. Would you like to spend the night with us? It's dry, and you get a hot meal!"

I liked that idea, and they asked about my plans. "Well, I teach school and have a degree in history, so I want to explore the Boston area. Lexington, Concord, Walden Pond, the USS *Constitution*. Boston played such a key role in starting our nation."

Once more the dad turned to his wife, this time with a longer and quieter personal discussion. "Please think about staying with us. We live just outside Boston. Use our house as a jumping-off point. We'd love to have you for meals, but don't feel you have to be here."

The next morning he left for work, leaving his wife and child alone with a long-haired, hippie, *Easy Rider* type. That blew me away. Whether or not they followed Jesus, they practiced some radical hospitality. Was that wise or biblical, or should we use caution? Before we say they got too involved in risky business, let's check it out with open minds.

Paul opened his letter to the Romans with theology—the divinity and humanity of Jesus, the necessity of the obedience of faith and more. Then, in chapter 12, he examines what theology means in daily life, how we should treat all people, both fellow followers and those who don't. Almost hidden in the abundance of actions is "Practice hospitality" (Romans 12:13).

Later, he extended our call: "Therefore, as we have opportunity, let us do good to all people" (Galatians 6:10). That sounds pretty inclusive. Paul made hospitality a requirement for church leaders (1 Timothy 3:2, Titus 1:8). An important trait, but then God slipped in a kicker.

"Be ready with a meal or a bed when it's needed. Why, some have extended hospitality to angels without ever knowing it!" (Hebrews 13:2 MSG). Think about the subtext—God sends angels to move among us, and we can't distinguish them from humans. That guy on the freeway that we cut off because we didn't want to wait our turn, that supermarket checker with whom we were rude—all these and more could be angels.

But it gets worse. Honest. Near the end of Matthew's gospel, Jesus gave the standards he uses to judge those who go up or those who go down. Basically, do we act in love to others like Jesus did?

> I was hungry and you gave me something to eat, I was thirsty and you gave me something to drink, I was a stranger and you invited me in, I needed clothes and you clothed me, I was sick and you looked after me, I was in prison and you came to visit me…Truly I tell you, whatever you did for one of the least of these brothers and sisters of mine, you did for me (Matthew 25:35-36,40).

Acts of hospitality. To those in need. Strangers. What we do to strangers we do to Jesus, and that determines our eternal destiny. Not on the basis of the acts, but because Jesus genuinely living in us expresses himself in hospitality.

And hospitality may come with risks. Jesus defined how to love our neighbors with the good Samaritan, where a traveler was beaten up by robbers and left half dead on a road that saw many ambushes. A priest came along and crossed to the far side of the road. Too risky, and he had important business. A Levite did the same. Then a hated alien, a Samaritan, from a mongrel race, came by, got off his donkey, bandaged the man, put him on his donkey, and took him to an inn. Having business to continue, he paid for future medical treatment and checked on the victim on his return (Luke 10:25-37).

Have no doubt, he faced risk. The wounded man could have been a decoy to get him to stop. Bending down to bandage him made him vulnerable. Traveling with the man on his donkey slowed him down, again increasing vulnerability. But he did it. A fellow human had a need and he could help—and did.

God doesn't want us to ignore risks; he told us to evaluate each event (1 Thessalonians 5:21) and to count the cost before we jump in

(Luke 14:28). We don't enable people to continue irresponsible behavior (2 Thessalonians 3:10). But he also told us to consistently act as an expression of faith: "Everything that does not come from faith is sin" (Romans 14:23). One caveat—my good Samaritan at Howard Johnson's consulted his wife, so don't put others at risk without their agreement.

But following Jesus comes with risks, not safety, according to C.S. Lewis: "If you want a religion to make you feel really comfortable, I certainly don't recommend Christianity."[1] It's not always safe to express faith in hospitality, but it is good.

KICK-STARTING THE APPLICATION

Before reading this, how strong was your commitment to hospitality? To risky hospitality? Has it changed? Why? Think of a time you passed up a chance to help someone. How do you now feel about it? Think of a time you expressed risky hospitality. How did it work out? What can you do to grow here?

5

WHEN ANGELS RIDE ALONG

Dealing with Danger

It all seemed so simple. After the movie *Easy Rider* captivated me as told in chapter 1, I bought the Honda 350 Scrambler, and three weeks later I launched for Canada.

Way too early, I knew almost nothing about riding or bikes. Not enough to know the danger.

As did nearly all bikes back then, the chain drive on my scooter needed daily maintenance—lubricating and tightening the chain. Well, I'd fallen in love with the unity of biker, bike, and the road. I did more riding than maintaining. The bike rode well, even though it was loaded high with a backpack strapped to the sissy bar. Pulling south out of Banff on Highway 93 in the magnificent Canadian Rockies, heading for Idaho, I took full advantage of the bike. Heading into a long, sweeping turn to the right, I barely noticed the 35 mph sign while doing at least 60. Okay, maybe more. Maybe a lot more.

But I had a good line—until the unmaintained chain slipped off the sprocket and locked the rear wheel. Mix a high center of gravity, a tight curve, and instant and complete braking with an inexperienced rider, and you have a recipe for going down hard. Not really knowing what to do, I somehow kept the bike upright until it skidded to a stop at the side of the road. After the adrenaline-induced shaking stopped, I took the bike half apart to get the chain off and back on. Needless to say, after that, not a day went by without the chain getting a little maintenance.

But I think I may have lied. I'm not sure I kept the bike up. Physics demanded a fall. A rookie rider almost guaranteed it.

God never spoke to me about this in a special message, but I'm convinced an angel—or several—kept the bike up that day above Radium Hot Springs. Humility may not be one of my greater gifts, but my minimal skills couldn't have kept the bike from sliding across the asphalt.

The obvious lesson: Maintain your gear. The more subtle one: A supernatural reality exists, independent of our belief in it. At that point in my life, I didn't follow God. I suspected the supernatural dimension was real, but I wouldn't have argued it. Six months later I did come back to God with no doubt about his power and involvement in our lives. This story played a role, because God stepped in to play a supernatural role. Before I believed.

Does God sometimes protect us supernaturally? I believe so. My story gives but one example. Read the first 35 verses of Hebrews 11, which has 28 separate occasions of people acting in faith. Thirteen of their faith actions involved supernatural action by God to bless or protect them. But continue with the last part of verse 35, where others, equally commended for their faith (verse 39), faced troubles.

Did angels ride along to save them? Not quite. They endured torture, jeering, beatings, chaining, imprisonment, stoning, being cut in two, killed by the sword, destitution, persecution, mistreatment, wandering, and living in caves and holes in the ground. Think of the New Testament apostles. Stephen, an early leader, was stoned to death—literally, not pharmacologically (Acts 7:54-59) and James the brother of John was assassinated (Acts 12:2). One verse later Peter landed in prison (12:3).

Why did some experience a supernatural rescue and others did not? Why does God sometimes rescue some of his people and not rescue others? I have no clue. I have thoughts and some explanations on a general basis. But on any individual case, I cannot know. But I do trust his love even more than I trust his power. I suspect that's the key. God's omniscience trumps our finite knowledge. I've seen enough of his love to have faith in it.

Out of his love he promises to work in all things for good. Whose good, though? Not necessarily our short-term preferences, but long-term good as God defines it. Honestly, that's a bit of a kicker. Short term, I want to stay upright on the bike. But I know God can give his comfort and presence and will work in all things. Even if I'd gone down.

So how do we deal with danger? We use all of our skills that we can. We get advice. We get support. We rely on God. And if he rescues us, we praise him. And if he doesn't, we praise him.

KICK-STARTING THE APPLICATION

Do you believe God intervenes supernaturally in our lives? Why or why not? To what extent do you think he works? Have you experienced times that you're pretty sure had a supernatural element, like my story? How did that impact you? How do you handle situations when God doesn't intervene? How deeply do you trust in God's love? What keeps you from growing that?

6

THE GLORY OF SILENCE

A Time to Pray

I've long said, as a sort of joke, that riding greatly increases my prayer life. And it should. A lot of idiots drive cars. Otherwise careful drivers just don't see bikes. Bikes trade away stability and protection for speed and maneuverability, which inherently increases the dangers we face. Bad weather can cause problems. And we all make mistakes. So I pray that God in his mercy will keep me safe. Or at least mobile and rational. But prayer plays another vital role in my riding.

In our core Gray Hogs group, two regularly listen to praise music or sermons as they ride. I suspect Jerry wouldn't be able to ride if he lost his Bluetooth connection. But two of us cruise in silence. No phone, no CB, no CDs, no smartphones. We enjoy the glory of quietness. I'm in this group, and that paid off on a trip to Washington.

I had planted a church in Temecula about eight years before, and we reached a good number of previously unchurched people. But we hit a plateau that we couldn't climb, finances were tight, exhaustion slowed me down, and I had no clue about our next step—should I resign and let the church find a new pastor? Should we beg or borrow enough to add a staff person? Should we close the doors? All of this came to a head just before a ride. That would provide a lot of time to pray and ponder away from daily distractions and responsibilities.

So I listed several dozen praise song titles on a card, attached it to the fairing, and loudly sang them on the first couple of days. Another benefit of riding—I don't damage the ears of others when I blast out in song. I just wanted to immerse myself in his presence. Frankly, I didn't pray a lot here, preferring to focus on enhancing our connection. The prayer came in the next stage. In conversations with God, we explored the history of the church, my gifts and weaknesses, future options, and a lot more.

And a result of days of this worship and prayer and pondering? Not a clue. Merely an overwhelming sense of God's presence and care, a connection that would carry me through whatever he brought or allowed to arrive. But on my first night home, I received a phone call from a leader of the church planting association we had been working with. Joe was leading a combination of three other small churches in the greater area. Would our church like to participate?

After a great deal of discussion with their group, our elders, and our congregation, the combination came together. The benefits: our church continued with fresh staff and a larger base of members and more financial support and I received a needed sabbatical. That sabbatical opened the door to writing, and I published my first book, a ministry venture that continues with this book, my tenth. This form reaches far more people than I could have dreamed of, especially if I had continued as pastor of that church.

Underlying the process—getting away, praying a lot, deepening and seeking God's presence. God created us like this, to get away at times. One example is the Sabbath day of rest, but how many of us truly practice it? Jesus also got away frequently, leaving the crowds and teaching and healing and miracles in order to restore his soul. So often, when we get away, it's a tightly scheduled vacation crammed with activities that only with difficulty do we hear God's whisper. Apart from this story, why is getting apart important?

First, God did it and commanded it. After the hard work of creating a universe, he kicked back: "By the seventh day God had finished the work he had been doing; so on the seventh day he rested from all his work. Then God blessed the seventh day and made it holy, because on it he rested from all the work of creating that he had done" (Genesis 2:2-3). Holy merely means separated from work. A time to rest and kick back. Not necessarily to be a slug, but to restore your soul. Like maybe a long bike trip.

And Jesus did it. I counted eight times that God recorded Jesus getting away from the crowds for solitude and prayer (Matthew 4:1, 8:18, 14:22, 15:39; Mark 3:7, 6:31, 6:46; John 6:15). The Son of God, fully divine in human form, needed solitude. Needed time with his dad. He loved crowds, drew them in and impacted them, but he didn't let the desires of others set his agenda. Not if it interfered with his connection with God.

In our fast-paced, success-oriented, demanding culture, we, too, need to set our spiritual agenda. At the very heart is getting unbusy. Getting away from stress and demands and hurry. Yes, that will cause tension as we make changes. Yes, that will likely upset others. But as part of the Ten Commandments we find: "Remember to observe the Sabbath day by keeping it holy. You have six days each week for your ordinary work, but the seventh day is a Sabbath day of rest dedicated to the LORD your God. On that day no one in your household may do any work" (Exodus 20:8-10 NLT).

Maybe we can decide to leave some margin in our lives as an antidote to busyness. Maybe we can avoid adding new activities and responsibilities unless we eliminate current ones that match the time and energy expended. Maybe we slow down enough to hear the quiet whispers of God. Maybe.

KICK-STARTING THE APPLICATION

Do you sometimes feel rushed or that your responsibilities are crushing you? If so, have you noticed a decreased ability to concentrate and hear God? How busy are you, and how much uncommitted time do you have each week? When you get away, do you tend to fill the days with nonstop activities? Do you regularly take some time away to just bask with God and listen to him?

7

GOOD GEAR

Gets You Where You Want to Go

Dad's genes ran true. When he was a teenager, he delivered telegrams in Los Angeles in the 1920s on a belt-drive Excelsior motorcycle. Guess I had no chance of avoiding bikes. One of many lessons I picked up from him applies to both bikes and cars: Have good tires.

With money tight in my early days of riding, I bought an inexpensive rear tire, put it on, and headed to work the next morning. The corner at Los Coyotes and Willow in Long Beach was easy, only about 45 degrees, and I'd made it hundreds of times. Except for this day. Halfway through the turn, the bike lost balance and almost slid down. I corrected it, but it crow hopped back and forth several times and I almost kept the bike up, until one crow hop caused a wheel to hit the curb, and I went down at about 5 mph. No damage to the bike, and I had just a slightly jammed left wrist.

So I cautiously headed home, drove my van to work, and returned the out-of-balance tire that night and bought a better one. Over 200,000 miles later, that's the only time I've gone down on the road. One reason—I learned the importance of good gear in riding safely.

That bad tire gives us a metaphor for riding with Jesus. We need good gear to reach our destination. For bikes that includes good tires, keeping the bike tuned and safe, helmets, and all. For the spiritual life that includes a number of items to have in our toolbox.

Unless we're a superwrench, having an owner's manual lets us best know how to ride and repair the bike. Particularly on my Honda ST1300 with all its bodywork, some guidance really helps. As followers, we need the same. We call it the Bible. I see it as God's owner's manual for life. After all, he created us and the world and the universe and best knows how they all function optimally.

Although the Bible doesn't answer all the questions we have, it gives the answers we need: "Jesus performed many other signs in the presence of his disciples, which are not recorded in this book. But these are written that you may believe that Jesus is the Messiah, the Son of God, and that by believing you may have life in his name" (John 20:30-31). What we most need, we have, *if* we access it. But if I need to replace the air cleaner, taking a look at how I need to loosen and lift the gas tank helps. Yet to do major engine work, you need more than the owner's manual.

Let me suggest that our basic owner's manual is a good, readable version of the Bible, like the New International Version (NIV) or New Living Translation (NLT). But for more intensive work get a shop manual or several different translations for our tool kit. A more literal word-for-word translation like the New American Standard Bible (NASB) or New King James Version (NKJV) is great, but add a handy paraphrase, like *The Message*. And a good study Bible, like the NIV Study Bible, has an abundance of notes, cross references, maps, and charts.

And the digital world gives an abundance of resources. I have a marvelous digital Bible, the Online Bible, that provides great resource tools. BibleGateway does the same, along with many Bible apps. Yeah, that involves some work and study, but we put that into our bikes, don't we?

Of all the guys I've ridden with, a couple fit into the category of close friends. Ones that speak truth to my folly, who will call me out on the issues. Once a key broke off in my gas cap lock and I couldn't find a locksmith, so I figured I'd ask my wife, Sheila, to overnight my extra key. The one at home. I told Mick and Brad to keep riding and I'd catch up with them as soon as I could.

They wouldn't leave, and we finally found a locksmith who somehow made a new key from the broken one. Brad had to ride back and forth between the shop and the bike to test the key. Probably eight times. I'll always remember these two friends. Spiritually, we need a few guys like that: "A man of many companions may come to ruin, but there is a friend who sticks closer than a brother" (Proverbs 18:24 ESV). In your journey with Jesus, be that kind of a friend who sticks around in hard times and cultivate some of your own.

Although there are four of us who form a core group of riders, I ride with a lot of guys. Several times with guys from the church. Or just guys I meet on a ride. I met Kevin at Shenandoah National Park a long time ago, shared a campsite one night, and we rode together for several days. Some ride with motorcycle clubs, like the HOGs (Harley Owners Group). Their commonality—a love of bikes.

The spiritual journey also needs to extend beyond a small core group to a larger one with a commonality of Jesus. We often call that a local church. It provides resources and opportunities that our small groups just can't. That connection builds depth when we don't just talk about rides but live life with each other, like the early church.

> They devoted themselves to the apostles' teaching and to fellowship, to the breaking of bread and to prayer. Everyone was filled with awe at the many wonders and signs performed by the apostles. All the believers were together and had everything in common. They sold their property and possessions to give to anyone who had need. Every day

they continued to meet together in the temple courts. They
broke bread in their homes and ate together with glad and
sincere hearts (Acts 2:42-46).

All followers need this type of connection, so, like with a bike, it's
important to do it. You only become a good rider if you ride. A lot.
The same with following Jesus. We live our faith. We get involved. We
use our gifts and talents and time to touch others for Jesus. We don't
leave our bikes parked in the garage.

Good destinations. Good gear. The two go together.

KICK-STARTING THE APPLICATION

Think about the tools for a spiritual tool kit. Which are you strong
in? What helped develop that? Think about the ones you need to grow
in more. What has kept you from developing there? What step can
you take this week to grow?

8

FRIENDLY FIRE

Dealing with Damage from Friends

We grew up in the same church in Long Beach, but Rich began riding bikes a few years before me, on a Honda 350. I soon bought a similar one, then Rich added a larger ride, a Harley Super Glide. Yeah, a few decades back. Despite being both friends and regular riding partners, or maybe because of it, we'd rag on each other's bikes—Rich defending Harleys, me defending Hondas. Okay, once his wife thought we were ready to break out the fists, but it was a friendly rivalry. Let's just call it spirited.

So when he T-boned me in Blythe, California, it was accidental, right? We'd left Prescott, Arizona, earlier and the temperature hit 113. We decided to stop at the first café for cold drinks. I was in the lead on the right side of the lane and saw a prospect on the left. I signaled and slowed and began to turn left. Rich, behind me in the left side of the lane, missed all of that.

Partway into the turn, my bike suddenly jumped sideways several feet. In the air. Rich's Harley had slammed into my Honda and I bounced. An angel must have held the bike up—I never went down, but my crash bar was bent at a 45-degree angle. A few inches closer to the front, the wheel gets hit and I go down. A few inches closer to the back, my leg gets hit and I go to the hospital. Yes, it *was* an accident, but it provided some evidence of Honda superiority for years: Takes a mauling but keeps on hauling. (Some call events like this friendly fire.)

A nice metaphor for church, isn't it? But some accidents with fellow followers don't always meet the description of "accidental." We get wounded, often knowingly. Just about all of us. Confidences get betrayed. Lies get told. Power struggles fracture friendships. Churches split over opinions. Friends never speak again. The list goes on and on. And often we withdraw from a partner in Christ, sometimes from the church itself.

Just last week our home group discussion focused on Judas's betrayal of Jesus, then we broke into men's and women's groups. Our leader asked if any of us had been betrayed and if we felt comfortable sharing the story. The openness of the men surprised me, but the shock deepened. Every betrayal was by a fellow Christian, several from years earlier, and the pain still ran deep. We're guys and no one cried, but it came close. We talked about how to reconcile, how to heal, how to confront, and how to find answers, but none were easy. I suspect we'll revisit our progress.

As followers of Jesus, how can we best respond to friendly fire? Let me suggest a few principles. Jesus' last prayer convicts me:

> I pray also for those who will believe in me through their message, *that all of them may be one*, Father, *just as you are in me and I am in you*. May they also be in us so that *the world may believe* that you have sent me. I have given them the glory that you gave me, that *they may be one as we are one*—I in them and you in me—so that they may be brought to *complete unity*. Then the world will know that you sent me and have loved them even as you have loved me (John 17:20-23).

Jesus wants unity for us all. Baptists, Presbyterians, Methodists, independents, any church, any group, any person who validly follows the Jesus of the Bible needs the same caliber of unity as seen in Jesus and the Father. That glory shouts the reality of God's ability to transcend troubles in a world badly in need of harmony.

Not only is the bar high, but it's critical that the world see believers united and in harmony. So here are several tips we can begin to implement in dealing with betrayal and friction and wounds:

1. Realize the betrayal and pain are real. Don't pretend it didn't happen. Pretending leads to more deception.

2. Realize some wounds can be ignored as momentary exceptions to an otherwise good relationship. Being imperfect, we'll all wound one another. Let mercy triumph over judgment and let it slide.

3. Realize some wounds cannot be ignored without allowing damage to grow. Here, speak the truth in love, offer forgiveness, and work toward reconciliation. Now, how can you tell the difference between this and the last? A lot of prayer and a lot of experience. Err on the side of openness and healing.

4. Realize not all fractures can be healed. Sometimes we must let go. Paul graces us here with this truth: "If it is possible, as far as it depends on you, live at peace with everyone" (Romans 12:18). We can't live at peace with all, but we can give it our best shot. Only then can we let it go.

Granted, these principles are brief and much easier to read than to practice. But we can't form a solid connection with God without solid connections with others, according to John: "Whoever does not love their brother and sister, whom they have seen, cannot love God, whom they have not seen" (1 John 4:20). That scares me deeply, so let's work on loving when it's difficult. Okay?

KICK-STARTING THE APPLICATION

Think about a few occasions when you've been wounded by friendly fire. What prompted the situation? Were you partially at fault or not at all? How did it affect you? How did it change the relationship? Were you able to reconcile? What most keeps you from reconciling with those who have wronged you?

Take some time to ponder and pray about a relationship that is now less than optimal because you caught some friendly fire. Can you take some steps to attempt to bring healing? What are they? Should you try? Does anything keep you from working on it?

9

RIDE FREE

Loosening Restrictions

Just after I graduated from college, I worked long enough to buy a Honda 350 Scrambler motorcycle and save a few bucks before taking off for Canada. My only objective: Visit a former roommate who had moved to Kamloops. No other plans, no watch. Just a few maps, some camping gear, and a little cash. The only time frame: Return for the start of grad school in late August.

Highway 1 began the adventure, following the coasts of California and Oregon and Washington, beginning near Malibu, through Big Sur and the redwoods of Northern California to the rocky ocean-side cliffs of Oregon and the verdant Olympic Peninsula, leading to Vancouver Island, the mountains of Canada, and then down to Montana, Yellowstone, and back home. But the route saw a lot of detours. Every intriguing sign, every interesting side road, every wild hair changed the path. Ten states, two provinces, two countries, 30 days, 6,000 miles, and my life changed. Not just that the glory of motorcycle touring hooked me, which it did. Not just that my appreciation for the beauty of open country grew, which it did. Not just that I found many exceptionally hospitable and helpful people, which I did.

But I learned a lot about freedom. About choices. Up to then, my life had been prescribed and regulated. Finish high school. Go to college. Work summers to save money for the next year at college. Get a good professional job. My life had been laid out.

But for the first time, I experienced genuine freedom.

Not merely the freedom of the open road, but freedom to choose what to do. Freedom to change course. Each side road became a metaphor of choice. I came very close to staying in Canada and skipping grad school entirely. From that trip I learned to ride free in life. To be flexible. To plan and to adapt. Can we live the Christian life this way? I like to think so.

Frankly, I struggled with that a bit for some time. The old Four Spiritual Laws told me "God loves you and has a wonderful plan for your life." Like many, I thought that meant he had the details all planned. The one woman in the world just right as my wife. The one profession that he chose for me. What if, in my freedom, I missed what God planned for me? What if I missed what my parents had planned? Or society? Or friends?

And if God does have just one specific plan for our lives, with each detail predetermined, then does choice have any meaning?

I came across a passage that totally changed how I viewed both life and following Jesus. Paul had traveled almost 200 miles, either on a slow boat or on foot, from Ephesus to Troas to preach to those who had never heard of Jesus—his passion. Upon his arrival, God opened a door to do that. God's will. Pretty clear.

Paul chose to ride free: "Now when I went to Troas to preach the gospel of Christ and found that the Lord had opened a door for me, I still had no peace of mind, because I did not find my brother Titus there. So I said goodbye to them and went on to Macedonia" (2 Corinthians 2:12-13). I expected a lightning bolt when Paul chose to ride free of God's open door.

Now, get the next verse: "But thanks be to God, who always leads us as captives in Christ's triumphal procession" (verse 14). Not only did the lightning not flash from heaven, making Paul a Post Toastee, but God approved.

God guides us. Sometimes quite clearly, and I have seen that repeatedly in my life and in the lives of others. He also allows us to choose and then blesses us in that. Okay, not so much when we choose sin, which we all understand, but to a large extent, we can ride free in life. We can make plans and change them on the fly. We can follow those plans. We can totally change them.

Let's return to God's plan for us. He does have one, the same for all of us. Every time I found a verse that definitely stated God's will for all people, that verse fit into just two topics. First, God's plan is that all freely choose to follow him, as in "The Lord is...longsuffering toward us, not willing that any should perish but that all should come to repentance" (2 Peter 3:9 NKJV). He wants us to walk with him in relationship.

God's plan continues once we choose to follow—he wants us HOLY to become godly, to be transformed into his own character: "It is God's will that you should be sanctified" (1 Thessalonians 4:3). Simply, being sanctified means that we cooperate with God as we become a new person with new values, new character, new hopes, and new behavior.

That encompasses God's plan. To know him, to follow him. Those areas are not negotiable. But beyond them, we can ride free. Let's do it wisely. Let's bathe it in prayer. But take confidence in God's belief that he can trust how we use our freedom.

KICK-STARTING THE APPLICATION

Have you experienced clear guidance? Have you experienced what you thought was clear guidance only to have things fall apart? Have you experienced, within the bounds of obedience to his commands, the freedom God gives to shape our lives? How did that work out? Does this concept of riding free change your view of God? Should it? How? What range of freedom do you see in the Christian life? How can you expand your concept of freedom and be faithful to God?

10

GRAB A GOAL

Your Own Personal Bucket List

I walked into the Kauai Harley-Davidson dealer in Lihue and surprised the salesperson. "Can I ride one of your bikes? Just for a block or so?"

"Uh, no. We don't do test rides. Insurance regulations won't allow it."

So I had to give the backstory. Several years ago a Facebook post asked you to list all the states you've visited, and it piqued my curiosity when I discovered I'd hit quite a few: 41 on just two wheels and 45 in all. Not too far from all 50. That sparked memories of the Morgan Freeman and Jack Nicholson movie *Bucket List*, where two terminal old farts decide to complete their wish lists before they kick the bucket.

I didn't have one. Didn't particularly care to craft one. But the idea of a one-item bucket list germinated, not to possess me, but as a target to shoot for. How about riding a motorcycle in all 50? I just needed Hawaii, Alaska, four states in the upper Midwest, and three in the Southeast. Forty-one done, nine to go. And here I was on vacation with my wife, sister, and brother-in-law with a chance to bag Hawaii.

"Well, I'd like to help, but…Wait a minute. Let me check."

He disappeared for a moment and came back with a set of keys. "We have a dirt bike we loan out to people who buy a bike to take the motorcycle road test on. How far again?"

"Just a block. I can do it in the parking lot."

He grinned. "Go for it," he said as he tossed me the keys.

I fired it up, drove once around the lot, and pulled in with a grin and thanks. One more state down, just eight to go. A few more have been added since then, with just four now left: Alaska, Georgia, South Carolina, and Florida. Kitty-cornering the country. Two more trips and…maybe. But all this sparked some serious thoughts.

What essential goals do I have for this journey through life? What goals should we all share? Spiritual bucket-list items vary between individuals, but these three we could all target, ones that will help us arrive where we desire with grins on our faces.

Knowing God should top the bucket list. According to Jesus, "This is eternal life: that they may know you, the only true God, and Jesus Christ, whom you have sent" (John 17:3). The concept of knowing God provides a central concept that all other facets radiate from. But the kicker comes with figuring out what that means. So I checked out the meaning of "know," written in Greek for a Jewish audience.

Now, don't get all weird here, but among the literal definitions— to know, to understand, to perceive—"know" is also a Jewish idiom for sexual intercourse. That is, intimacy. A moment-by-moment connection between two beings. Not primarily behavior or attending church, but a relationship. Heart-to-heart sharing.

Too often we imagine that saying we follow, and doing some good things for God, means we know him. But that's not quite right. According to Jesus:

> Not everyone who says to me, "Lord, Lord," will enter the
> kingdom of heaven, but only the one who does the will of

my Father who is in heaven. Many will say to me on that
day, "Lord, Lord, did we not prophesy in your name and in
your name drive out demons and perform many miracles?"
Then I will tell them plainly, "*I never knew you*. Away from
me, you evildoers!" Therefore everyone who hears these
words of mine and puts them into practice is like a wise
man who built his house on the rock" (Matthew 7:21-24).

*To know—
but not
be known.*

Yeah, a tough passage. We can do the right stuff, but if we don't
know Jesus personally, it doesn't matter. And if we genuinely know
him, then we will do the right stuff. Not perfectly, but we should
be improving. So if you're not there now and would like to be, just
stop and ask him to enter your life as Lord and Savior, and then start
following.

And begin reshaping your values to match his. Reshape your character, your actions. A good start on your spiritual bucket list.

2) A second target is to love all people: "Whoever claims to love God
yet hates a brother or sister is a liar. For whoever does not love their
brother and sister, whom they have seen, cannot love God, whom
they have not seen" (1 John 4:20). If we love God, we love his people.
The good ones who ride the same bike we do. The bad ones who ride
a different bike. But we don't need to feel warm fuzzies. That's liking,
and we don't have to do that. Simply put, love acts in the best interests of the person we love. Like God: "God so loved the world that he
gave..." (John 3:16). He acted to benefit us.

Now, let's put these two bucket lists together to get more practical. From our first bucket item, the most essential goal in life is making the choice to know and to follow God. If we love an individual,
then we act to help them make those decisions. Decisions that bring
them to know and more fully follow. We can't force them. They must
decide. But part of our bucket list is to impact people positively so

they'll make those decisions. Frankly, we don't have just one way to do this. But it's on the bucket list!

(3) Third, be nice. I hope people remember me as one of the good guys. Not perfect but growing. Acknowledging my wrongs and failings. Yeah, plural on both. That's a good goal for us all, and it really flows out of the last one we explored: to act in love to people. We may not tell them about Jesus overtly, but they should see Jesus in us. We call that expressing the Spirit: "The fruit of the Spirit is love, joy, peace, forbearance, kindness, goodness, faithfulness, gentleness and self-control. Against such things there is no law" (Galatians 5:22-23). They may outlaw being a Christian, telling people about Jesus. But they're not likely to outlaw being nice.

So a suggested bucket list. Yeah, I'm still going for the 50. But these three are the real things.

KICK-STARTING THE APPLICATION

Do you have a bucket list? What are some key goals? Do you have a spiritual bucket list? If not, why not? If you do, what are some key elements? What do you think of the three suggested here? Think about each and evaluate how well you're doing. How can you move closer to your bucket list goals this week? Will you?

11

LIVE WELL

Enjoying God's Gifts

Mid-September and the end of a three-month motorcycle tour of the United States grew near. Money had begun to run low, and Denver had just gotten snow. Heading toward Aspen from the east, I came across my personal campground, open but deserted with the onset of the fall that comes early to the high country. Gold already adorned the aspen, and a likely looking trout stream ran next to my site. Lacking a license but unable to resist some temptations and relying on the solitude, I threw in a line. Not much time elapsed before I landed a decent-sized rainbow. Dinner. Living off the land.

Earlier I'd picked up some artisan bread and plums. I baked the trout in the embers of the campfire. Leaning against an aspen, I enjoyed as fine a meal as I'd consumed the entire trip. Well, the flounder stuffed with crab in New Orleans might have matched the meal, but not the ambiance. Even though I'm a pathetic musician, I pulled out a harmonica and tried to match the tune of the stream as it ran to the sea. Since the evening came so near to perfection, the harmonica was put away so the stream's beauty could continue uninterrupted.

So what does this have to do with spiritual formation? First, God has provided a marvelous world that he designed for us to enjoy. Some of us battle a puritanical streak that almost assumes our pleasure can't please God. I've jokingly said that some experiences are so pleasurable they must be sinful. Well, mostly joking. But that denies God's goodness and desire to bless us.

Take a look at just some of the verses that support God's wanting us to enjoy the world, food, and fun:

"God said, 'Let us make human beings in our image, to be like us. They will reign over the fish in the sea, the birds in the sky, the livestock, all the wild animals on the earth, and the small animals that scurry along the ground'" (Genesis 1:26 NLT).

"I decided there is nothing better than to enjoy food and drink and to find satisfaction in work. Then I realized that these pleasures are from the hand of God" (Ecclesiastes 2:24 NLT).

"Go ahead. Eat your food with joy, and drink your wine with a happy heart, for God approves of this!" (Ecclesiastes 9:7 NLT, see also 2:25, 3:13, 8:15).

When we enjoy these blessings, we better connect with the God who gave them for our pleasure. We sense his love. We feed our souls when we live well (not necessarily extravagantly but well). That meal may have cost just a few dollars, but the ambiance and flavor and peacefulness surpassed the best New York restaurant. Enjoy the physical aspects of the life that God has provided. At times we must sacrifice, so sacrifice and smile. At other times we sit back and take pleasure in the world we're given. Both are normal, okay, and needed.

Obviously, follow his word as we do this. Too much enjoyment of food leads to gluttony and health risks. Too much enjoyment of wine leads to drunkenness. And some pleasures bring more damage than joy—God calls those sins.

Second, find what feeds your unique soul. My wife's soul, in that same spot, would experience sacrifice, not pleasure. But give her a luxury hotel with room service, and the smiles arrive. Our uniqueness springs from our DNA to experiences to personalities to spiritual gifts. *Sacred Pathways* by Gary Thomas explores some of the varied ways we feed our soul. Pick it up and digest it, you'll benefit.

I need regular mountain and outdoor fixes to restore me to humility and grace. Riding contributes to that. Figure out what works best for you in connecting to God and his creation. Since many of us enjoy riding bikes, view them as gifts from God. Dirt bikes. Sport bikes. Cruising bikes. Touring bikes. Multisport bikes. Let the pleasure you feel in riding remind you of his care.

KICK-STARTING THE APPLICATION

Has riding your bike enhanced your connection with God? How does that work for you? Apart from riding, what have you found from God's creation that best brings you pleasure? Do you consciously connect that pleasure with God? Why or why not? Have you viewed pleasure as good or bad or neutral? Why?

Let's pursue that tangent. What best connects you with God? Daily devotions? Praise music? Nature? Fellowship? Serving? What in those makes it work for you? What does that tell you about yourself? Pragmatically, what can you do to enhance your chances to connect with the grace of God's creation more frequently and deeply?

12

AN EARNED RESPECT

Responding to Authoritarianism in Authorities

Back in 1974 this long-haired hippie biker rode a semichopped 750 Honda with an *Easy Rider* American flag paint job into Groton, Connecticut, in the late afternoon, intending to spend the night and see the sights the next day, particularly nearby Mystic Seaport. After riding a few blocks, I noticed a police cruiser slide in behind me. It stayed right there. So I turned right. It did too. Another block brought a left turn. The cruiser turned too.

Recognizing the inevitable reality, I pulled over, ready to be hassled. I turned the bike off, put down the kickstand, and kept my empty hands on the handlebars. A Utica cop about a week before had pulled me over for no cause and even took me to the police station before his partner cut me loose. The Groton cruiser stopped behind me, and the cop got out and walked up to my bike.

"Hello, I'm Officer Sanders. I saw you ride into town and didn't recognize your bike. If you're new in this area, I'd love to do anything I can to help you enjoy our town."

That struck me dumb. His obvious pleasantness amazed me. We ended up having a great conversation. He'd recently moved to Groton from New York and was a fine guy. I told him my plans to see Mystic and then asked a favor. Remember, he'd volunteered.

"Is there a place I can throw my sleeping bag on the ground tonight that's acceptable and safe?"

He suggested a nearby park and told me where to park the bike and where to put the bag. We parted, I checked out the park, went out and got dinner, and after dark rode back and settled in for the night. All was well with the world. Until a car pulled into the park and the headlights pointed right at me. A bit hard to sleep like that, then a gruff voice shouted, "Get out of the bag!"

I mumbled "What do you want?" as I fumbled for a knife for protection from what I feared might be an imminent attack.

Then the guy turned on some flashing lights. A cop. An angry one. "I said, get out of the bag!" Fortunately, I hadn't found the knife, got up, and he walked over. "What are you doing here?" Not another friendly Groton cop.

I explained that I taught school, was exploring America and Mystic, and that Officer Sanders said I could sleep here. I suspect only Officer Sanders held any weight. He finally gave up, saying, "Well, don't mess up the place," and huffed off.

One day. Two local law enforcement officers. One good, one not so good. That forced me to ponder, as a follower of Jesus, about respecting those who don't earn respect. And what I found distressed me a bit.

First, what does it mean? Scripture commands followers to respect government leaders (Romans 13:7), wives to respect their husbands (Ephesians 5:33), workers their employers (Ephesians 6:5), and all of us to be ready to tell others about Jesus (1 Peter 3:15). In these, the original word is *phobos*, meaning "fear." Another verse commands that church members should respect church leaders (1 Thessalonians 5:12), but it uses the word *oida*, meaning "to know," "to perceive," or "to recognize." And *time*, in Greek, occurs twice: to respect all people (1 Peter 2:17) and for husbands to respect their wives (1 Peter 3:7),

which means to honor and value. Basically, we should respect all people. And nothing here gives us an out if they don't deserve respect.

Let's put that all together. Because of a person's innate worth, we
need to value them. If they have a leadership role, we recognize that
position and realize they have power that can touch our lives. Please
don't think that means we fall at their feet and worship them—we all
share a fallen humanity, and some are more fallen. Even cops. And
presidents. And pastors. And we don't always have to agree with them.
But in our disagreement, we must remain respectful.

Now, what if they don't earn respect (like the second Groton cop)?
We still honor their position. We honor the value that God places on
them as human beings. We speak respectfully. We don't scorn or slam
them. And this is the part I struggle with. We disagree agreeably. Let
me give two reasons for that.

First, God wants us to do that. Paul disagreed often with the religious and political leaders he encountered, but he did so with civility.
And Jesus said, in Matthew 25:40, that how we treat others equates to
how we treat him: "Truly I tell you, whatever you did for one of the
least of these brothers and sisters of mine, you did for me." So God
cares, deeply, that respect flows from our lives.

Second, this works in practice. In the Groton park, if I'd responded
with anger and scorn and insults, where I spent the rest of the night
would likely have been very different. In the midst of our political disagreements, perhaps we can disagree with respect rather than slam-
ming the character of the person with whom we disagree. The same
applies to talking with cult members who come to our front door.
Invite them in, offer them a refreshing drink, and open a respectful
conversation about truth.

But what if an authority requires us to do something that violates
Scripture? We follow God and accept the consequences. When some
Jewish leaders commanded that Peter not talk about Jesus, he simply

responded, "We must obey God rather than human beings!" (Acts 5:29). And sometimes Peter went to prison for that. As did Paul. But they both made a clear distinction: We follow God first and treat all with respect even when they don't behave in a manner that deserves it.

KICK-STARTING THE APPLICATION

Think about a recent disagreement you've had, either personal or political. Would the other person have mostly sensed respect or scorn? What most keeps you from consistently expressing respect? Have you ever thought of how you treat someone equates to how you treat Jesus? How will you change this week in how you express respect for all?

13

FLASHES OF GLORY

Unexpected Glimpses of God

In a lifetime of following Jesus, with a plethora of peaks and valleys, of feasts and feathers, I've learned that managing expectations determines the level of faith frustration or satisfaction. Unrealistic hopes, when birthed, tend to result in disappointment with God—a jaded "been there, done that" experience.

Here's the lesson I learned.

Flashes of Glory

Only when riding east to work
Only at the proper time of year
* when the sun's position on its north-south journey*
* aligns with the angle of the 101*
Only at the proper time of day
* when the sun rises*
* to just the right height above the horizon*
Only when I glance behind the bike
* through the side mirrors*
* at just the correct instant*
Only then
* do the Botts' dots that divide the lanes*

> *reflect the sun's light into a string of red rubies*
> *marking my trail*
> *Only that often*
> *do all the aspects of my life*
> *burst into glory*
> *And I can live with that*
> *as long as I arrive*

Until we moved to Thousand Oaks, where I occasionally drove to work my vintage Honda Gold Wing or the Kawasaki Vulcan 900LT that replaced it, I'd never experienced the above. But I'd been taking my newer Honda ST1300 in much more, and I do tend to look around a lot, both for scenery and safety. The Botts' dots have a red reflector on the upstream side. The idea: If you're a bit confused by too much of some substance or lack of sleep or possess suicidal thoughts, and you then enter the freeway going in the wrong direction and don't notice hundreds of cars speeding toward you, then you will see the red Botts' dots reflecting your headlights. If that happens at night. Daytime, you better look out for the oncoming cars and pay attention to them.

But last spring I saw this and again this fall. When all is just right, the sun bounces off the red reflectors, and you can see them *if* you're looking back at the right moment during a perfect timing of certain conditions. Like I said, it's rare. But the reflected red rubies behind add a touch of glory to a morning ride to work. And I need that boost on workdays.

Those red rubies are as rare as when life comes together in glory. Hope for them, pray for them, but don't expect them every day, or frustration will gnaw at your soul.

Jesus promised troubles would attack us, one of those promises we tend to ignore (John 16:33). Jesus promised temptations would batter us (Luke 17:1). Life includes trouble and pain and disappointment.

But the Lord provides the resources we need to handle them, and they will come, even as we wish for Botts' dots.

And sometimes we have no big issues, and our lives have become mundane. Life is boring. There's no flash, no pizzazz. After all, we can't ride all the time. We've settled into a rut while yearning to live on a mountaintop.

We desire those road rubies every day. They exist. But their glory seems to be proportional to their rarity. That rarity brings frustrations, when we cry that we didn't sign up for this or we reject faith because Jesus didn't do what we wanted him to do. A loved one isn't healed and doubt develops. A raise isn't given and bitterness eats at us. A ministry job goes to another and jealousy slips into our hearts. We want the stuff of Jesus' times, not blasé lives.

Maybe we're looking at and hoping for the wrong result, namely, our preferences rather than God's goals for us and his overall mission. Years ago I heard author Keith Miller assert that success in life comes from two realizations: God is real and we're not him. Sometimes, we need to let God be God and rest in him through the difficulties and dreariness that come our way.

We want the rubies. The good times. The ease. The great achievements. But did he promise these? Do these compose the normal Christian life? Maybe we need to accept the reality that the rubies are rare and that very rarity makes them even more special. Maybe we need to move down from the mountaintop to the valleys below. To be content with serving him and leaving the results to him.

Years back, when contemplating and praying about entering the ministry, I came across a passage that took a lot of pressure off. I realized we're not responsible for results, just serving the best we can. Paul said, "I planted the seed, Apollos watered it, but God has been making it grow. So neither the one who plants nor the one who waters is anything, but only God, who makes things grow" (1 Corinthians 3:6-7).

Can we trust in his amply demonstrated love? Can we rely on his wisdom as shown in a marvelously intricate and complex and orderly world? Can we be confident that he is working in the world for good, as he had done for millennia? This doesn't minimize the very real pain and suffering many go through or even ordinary lives. Rather, it maximizes the reality that God is here. He knows. He cares. And we can manage our expectations to take better advantage of all God is.

Every so often, if our eyes are open and we look closer, we'll see those flashes of ruby glory, those unexpected glimpses of God.

KICK-STARTING THE APPLICATION

Do you tend to get frustrated with God's not coming through on your prayers or expectations? Why? What has caused that? Does your life seem odd, ordinary, dull, drab? Take a little time to explore what you expect from God. Don't get sidetracked by what you hope for but what would disappoint you if it didn't come. Key question: Do you expect your wishes and requests or the actual, clear promises he's made? How can you tell the difference?

When it is a valid promise, what role does patience play? Do you have a pattern of thinking God does things late, like a college student, after a late night, strolling into class 15 minutes after the lecture's begun? How would your walk with Jesus change if you decreased your expectations as to what he's promised?

14

RIDING EQUALS WORSHIP

Moving Beyond a Six-Foot Perspective

Riding equals worship. Why? Because it pushes me beyond a human approach to life. Okay, that may not make sense yet, so let me explain the process.

I tend to see the world through a six-foot perspective—the average height of men my age, although I'm an inch short on that one. When I'm in a crowd, I often judge if I'm taller than most or shorter. Frequently I come out ahead—pardon the pun.

This perspective was embedded in me as a Boy Scout. They taught us to measure the height of a tree (or any height, like the peak of a roof) by having a six-foot person stand in front of it, then hold an arm straight out, with a thumb raised, and see what spot on the thumb matched his height. Then you count the number of times it takes for this to reach the top. Multiply by six, and you get pretty close to the real height.

But six feet represents more than just height; it's a worldview. I tend to evaluate life and others from my own near-six-foot perspective. Or from my own humanity, my own egocentrism. I'm the standard I use to evaluate life and people. How can this person benefit me? How will this impact my life? Do I fit into this group of people?

And a six-foot perspective justifies this for me. I suspect many others do this as well. (I'm not as unique as I once liked to think.)

Let's take this a step further. If a six-foot perspective also drives our values as a society, then we can evaluate options, at least on a short-term basis, by how they benefit people on the whole. Are gas prices too high? Then let's use oil extraction methods that might endanger the environment. After all, the earth is supposed to benefit us, right? Why should America cut back on carbon-dioxide emissions if other major economic powers don't? We'd be at a disadvantage.

A six-foot perspective can justify all of that and more. Which is why I ride.

On a ride to Glacier National Park, I put on about 600 solo miles the first day. One man, one day, 600 miles. But a six-foot perspective is shattered by scale. I rode 3,168,000 feet that day. Or 528,000 people, each six-feet tall, laid end to end. Suddenly, that six-foot perspective doesn't quite work. For the overall trip, covering 4,000 miles, that was 21.1 million feet. How many hypothetical people? Three and a half million.

So I get home and my wife asks how far we rode. "Oh, a few more than three million people." Ridiculous.

Let's get more ridiculous. In my 49 years of riding, I've put on more than 240,000 miles. That's equivalent to 1.7 billion people laid end to end. A six-foot perspective can't work on a greater scale. It seems pretty big on just a human level. But it breaks down when applied to the massive size of our earth.

One more thought: A six-foot perspective shatters any sense of absolute morality or values. If I'm the standard, then I can justify anything I'm able to do and get away with. You can do the same. So can we all. And the result? Chaos. So our worldview must change.

I ride, long distances sometimes, for that reason. Long rides force me to realize I'm not the be-all and end-all; I'm pretty puny in comparison to the earth. And frankly the earth is pretty puny compared to some other planets in our solar system, our galaxy, our universe. Covering miles, seeing the massiveness of mountains and the barrenness of deserts, doesn't fill me with pride at my accomplishments. I need the humility that comes with scale. If six feet is the standard, I look pretty good. Compared to thousands of miles, compared to the majesty of mountains, compared to the vastness of stars, my ego shrinks quickly.

I find it impossible to think this meticulously balanced earth and universe came about by chance. David shared my sense of awe: "The heavens declare the glory of God; the skies proclaim the work of his hands. Day after day they pour forth speech; night after night they display knowledge. There is no speech, they use no words; no sound is heard from them" (Psalms 19:1-3).

Wherever we go, the Creation proclaims the existence of the Creator. And a particular type, according to Paul: "Since the creation of the world God's invisible qualities—his eternal power and divine nature—have been clearly seen, being understood from what has been made, so that people are without excuse" (Romans 1:20). Only a being of tremendous power and a transcendent divine nature could craft all this.

So how do we stack up with this perspective? A combination of exceptional humility and a surprising twist. "When I consider your heavens, the work of your fingers, the moon and the stars, which you have set in place, what is mankind that you are mindful of them, human beings that you care for them?" (Psalm 8:3-4). David's realization that we just don't measure up to God or his creation is like the humility I feel when I'm weaving through the mountains.

But that's not the end of the story! David continues: "You made them a little lower than the angels and crowned them with glory and honor. You made them rulers over the works of your hands; you put everything under their feet" (verses 5-6). He loves us. He values us.

Doesn't God, being this kind of God, know best how people live? He made us. And he brings a moral order out of the chaos.

We call this worship. "Worthyship." Acknowledging that God's worth exceeds us in every way. Recognizing that he values and loves us and wants a relationship. See what I meant, riding equals worship?

KICK-STARTING THE APPLICATION

Like me, have you tended to let yourself be the standard of right and wrong? How has that worked for you overall and in relationships? Have you equated riding with worship before? What most connects you with God when you ride? What can you look for in your next ride that will reveal God and his majesty?

15

GETTING CLEAN

Seeing Stress Blow Away in the Breeze

When I was cruising through the Deep South on my Honda 750, the abundance of greenery startled me. Rolling hills covered with trees and moss, small farms, a few large plantations, all under a crystal-blue sky. With the temperature and humidity both around 100, riding in a tank top seemed a necessity. A nice necessity back in the days when we loved to bake and broil under the summer sun for the sake of getting a tan. And then, out of nowhere, a mass of bugs attacked my bare skin, which was moving along at about 70 mph with no windscreen. They stung. And stuck. Unlike most bugs that hit and run, they stuck. To my shirt. My arms. My face. My bike. I thought these bugs must have been the source of Super Glue.

I pulled over and popped on my jacket for protection, and a Mississippi River of sweat started to stream off my body. Just no way to win. At the next gas station, I cleaned my bug-covered headlight and asked the attendant what he knew about the flying beasts.

"Oh, yeah, we call them love bugs. They come in pairs during the mating season. Guess you can figure out why."

"Any way to avoid them?"

He grinned at this California biker. "Nope."

In my early solo trips, I usually camped out, but nowadays I enjoy a decent hotel with a hot shower and a soft bed. Even with a fairing, you need to clean off the day's road grime, and the hot water soothes sore muscles. The old line has some truth: You can tell a happy biker by the bugs in his teeth.

It's a paradox, though, how to ride to get rid of stress while riding deposits layers of dirt and bugs that need to be washed away.

Life just comes with stress. Granted, we cause some of it, but some of it lands on us like those love bugs. We just happen to be in a good place at a bad time. Studies abound about the problems caused by stress, and having a workable definition helps. The editors at Merriam-Webster define it as "a state of mental tension and worry caused by problems in your life, work, etc., something that causes strong feelings of worry or anxiety."[1] They seem to have been reading my journal!

I recently ran across this line: "Feeling stressed? Maybe you just need an iron supplement." A picture of a bike accompanied it. Yeah, the iron horse. Let's check out three stress solvers that work on our iron horses.

First, enjoy the wind. Although I can't explain this, despite the bugs and road grime, riding cleanses us of stress. A lot of bikers will say you'll never see a bike parked outside a psychiatrist's office. Part of this comes from the freedom of the open road, part from the wind carrying stress away. But some recent studies have gone deeper. The Ryuta Kawashima Laboratory of the Department of Functional Brain Imaging, Institute of Development, Aging and Cancer at Tohoku University studied riders and nonriders and concluded that regular riding stimulates the right prefrontal cortex functions, increases thinking functions overall, and also improves mental health, particularly stress reduction.[2]

In part, we concentrate more, which lessens stress. Maybe our concentration on riding pushes out the thoughts of our worries and cares. But we can take it a step further by following God's command to David: "Be still, and know that I am God!" (Psalm 46:10). With the normal benefit of riding, as the wind takes away stress, we intentionally choose to connect with God. We relax mentally and emotionally with him. We become more aware of his presence. God promises the more still we are, the more we will know him. What a reason to ride!

Second, use that improved thinking to analyze and ponder and pray. Think about this: When we ride, we think more effectively, so let's take advantage of it. Long ago Socrates said "the unexamined life is not worth living."

So let's check out our lives as we ride. That's biblical, "Let us examine our ways and test them, and let us return to the LORD" (Lamentations 3:40). Only as we ponder our lives can we fully walk with God. We find the sources of our sins and deal with them. We explore dysfunctional relationships and discover how we might improve them or deal with their reality. Maybe we think about what stresses us, how we invited it in, what options we have to deal with it. We ask God for insights. Maybe, when we stop, we ask our fellow riders for their ideas.

Third, rest in God. Being in his world helps. We see the world he created, its beauty and detail and massiveness. We see the intricate design that causes all of it to work together. And when stress arrives, we choose either to rely on our own abilities or his. This passage gives a solution, one that we may not like: "My heart is not proud, LORD; my eyes are not haughty; I do not concern myself with great matters or things too wonderful for me. But I have calmed and quieted myself, I am like a weaned child with its mother; like a weaned child I am content" (Psalm 131:1-2).

Unresolved problems cause stress. So how should we respond? We see the majesty of God's creation and remember that he is fully capable. On matters too great for us to do anything, ones we can't get our minds around, we choose calm and quiet our souls and rest in God.

We don't get angry at things we can't change. We don't let disappointment drive us. We rest in God's hands with the peace of a child being held by its mother.

So you want to blow that stress away? Hop on and ride.

KICK-STARTING THE APPLICATION

What's the level of stress in your life? What is in your power to change? On the issues you can't change, how do you handle them? Anger? Frustration? Resting in God's arms? In looking at the three stress cleansers, how can you use them on your next ride?

16

MIX FUN WITH SERVING

Both Express God's Heart

Back in my early twenties, I led an informal group that traveled to Mexico to work at the Tijuana Christian Mission, which included an orphanage in Tijuana. Not long before I had attended a college conference in nearby San Diego that featured a day trip there. The level of poverty astounded this middle-class guy, and God touched my heart. So about once a month, half a dozen of us headed south to play with the kids, build the walls of a house, play with the kids, build a roof for the house, play with the kids...well, you get the picture.

Yes, it involved some sacrifice. An entire weekend for single folk. Camping gear to take along. Food to cook. We paid for the construction materials. Ironically, we still felt selfish, even though we'd discovered the joy of serving. But one simple experience challenged me to a better understanding of following Jesus.

Sergio, the founder of the mission, knew I rode. One day he said, "Tim, I need to go pick up some paperwork, and I have two Triumph bikes. Wanna take a ride?"

I hadn't dreamed of how well road bikes could function as dirt bikes with the mere addition of knobby tires and the deletion of unnecessary parts. Sergio led me on a dirt adventure over hills and down valleys, jumping every slight rise, popping wheelies just for fun. At the time I had a 350 Honda Scrambler, and these 650cc Triumphs amazed me with their power and maneuverability. I had exclusively ridden on roads, but these dirt roads opened a new world of two-wheel fun for me.

That night, however, guilt began to seep in. I had abandoned my coworkers and had fun while they labored. But it went deeper. We came here to serve. To work. To sacrifice. At that young age, I saw the world in black and white, with not enough experience and thought-fulness to understand the concept of paradox (two contradictory ideas that are simultaneously true).

Ministering required sacrifice. I got that and willingly gave. But pleasure seemed suspiciously too close to sin. How could these be combined at the same time? Yeah, pretty immature. But real. That day of serving and pleasure expanded my thoughts. Serving is good. Pleasure is good. When we do both correctly. But how?

Serving Is Essential

For many of us, desiring our own way most interferes with spiritual growth. Adam and Eve shared that weakness, so we get it honestly. But God provided a couple of tools to combat it. Worship focuses on the greatness of God; it helps us realize God is real and we're not him. But serving others works in the same way. We become more Christ-like as we deny the preeminence of our desires by serving others. We raise their needs to the level of our own.

Jesus made that clear: "Whoever wants to become great among you must be your servant, and whoever wants to be first must be your slave—just as the Son of Man did not come to be served, but to serve, and to give his life as a ransom for many" (Matthew 20:26-28).

When we serve, we follow the example of Jesus. Rather than allow our desires to drive us, we sacrifice what we'd prefer to benefit others.

Pretty countercultural, right? But Jesus' brother James took it even further and was very specific about whom we should serve: "Religion that God our Father accepts as pure and faultless is this: to look after orphans and widows in their distress" (James 1:27).

There was no safety net in Judea in the first century, not like what we have in the United States today. So the most vulnerable people of the first century were orphans and widows. What faith does God see as genuine? To care for the disadvantaged. Yes, we can try to meet the needs of everybody, but perhaps we need a special focus on the most needy around us.

Like Jesus did. And yes, that involves sacrifice. For Jesus, he gave his life to serve us. Most of us won't be called to do that, but it summarizes what it means to follow Jesus.

But sometimes we can go too far. We can neglect our needs so much we can't really help others. We can slide into codependency. We can allow serving to become a sense of superiority. So just as serving balances egocentrism, God also provides an antidote to this.

Have Fun

In SoCal, lawns grow year-round. So one recent January day, I pulled out my lawn mower. Clear blue sky, temperature about 64, and I enjoyed the glory of the world God gave us. While mowing. God wants us to have fun, to take pleasure in the material world. Like riding stripped-down Triumphs. "*I commend the enjoyment of life*, because there is nothing better for a person under the sun than to eat and drink and be glad. Then joy will accompany them *in their toil* all the days of the life God has given them under the sun" (Ecclesiastes 8:15).

Look for material pleasures. God gave them for that purpose. And notice that Solomon's advice combines pleasure (riding a Triumph) with work (serving at an orphanage). God designed us for both, and we can't craft a whole life without both. It's okay to take a break from serving and have fun. But we can take the pursuit of pleasure or serving too far.

Out-of-balance pleasure hinders our spiritual growth, "The seed that fell among thorns stands for those who hear, but as they go on their way they *are choked by life's worries, riches and pleasures,* and they do not mature" (Luke 8:14). I've seen how focusing on pleasure has hurt my walk with God. It can also hurt our enjoyment of the material world: "Whoever loves pleasure will become poor" (Proverbs 21:17).

So hop on a bike and enjoy it and the world. But serve people along the way.

KICK-STARTING THE APPLICATION

How well do you include serving in your life? Should you increase or decrease it? How well do you include pleasure in your life? Should you increase or decrease it? How well do you balance the two? How can you improve that balance?

17

THE ROLE OF RULES

Learning to Trust the Creator

Back in the early '70s, my friend John and I led a month-long mission trip to Penasco, New Mexico, just outside Taos, and helped with the recreation program in the village. We had a diverse crew. Three from Purdue met six of us from various cities in southern California. Our caravan consisted of a van and two bikes as we journeyed across the deserts and mountains and rivers, enjoying the open road.

Both bikes looked cool and custom. I rode a 750 Honda with an extended front end, an *Easy Rider* American flag paint job, a custom seat, and a sissy bar. Other than those things, the bike was basically how the factory made it. Joe's bike had a 750 Honda motor and was totally custom and totally cool, winning the foreign show bike competition at that year's Winternationals.

From New Mexico, I rode to Nashville to see family, covering about 5,000 miles for the overall trip. The only problem came when a piece of grit was caught in the carburetor jets and took half an hour on the side of the road to fix.

Joe had a different story. Outside Williams, Arizona, he quickly braked and pulled to the side of the highway with a blown tire. His tightly fitted rear fender looked great in the show, but attaching the license plate left a small round-headed bolt on the bottom that rubbed the tire on every bump. His tire blew out after 800 miles. That required a fast ride with John on the back of my bike to Flagstaff before the shop closed for the weekend. Fortunately, we made it. John's job was to hold the new tire on the way back, and he still grins at the memory.

The next day, riding at about 75, Chris began to swerve in his lane, trying to raise his seat from the bike's seat. But with no lower foot pegs and only highway pegs, he had almost no ability to stand. Bad wiring had caused the battery to overheat, which warmed the bike's seat considerably. He made it to Penasco, but only after hours of work on his bike each day. And when he was heading home, somewhere between Penasco and SoCal, his bike broke down. Unrideable. The custom bike arrived home in the back of a pickup.

That made me think a lot about bikes. Honda engineers have a lot of education and expertise at building bikes, and my basically stock 750 showed it. The next summer I covered 31 states and 13,000 miles on a three-month trip with *no* problems. The design functioned. But then some nimrod said, "I want a kicked-out front end with a radical rake, a peanut gas tank, concealed wiring, and a cool paint job." Although it looks good, it can't perform as well. It abandons the experts' original design.

Our lives are like that. Many of us see following Jesus as our having to follow a lot of rules, which I did early on. These rules restrict our choices, and we see God as a cosmic spoilsport who wants to take away all the fun in life. But somewhere between birth and death, following rules breaks down. Rules ruin relationships.

We need to change our paradigm, not just for riding, but for life, for following Jesus. A new understanding that demonstrates the reality of God's rules balanced with the positive benefits of our obedience. Honda's engineers want to provide the best riding experience.

The closer we follow their design, the better we ride. God wants to provide our best life experience. The closer we follow his design, the better we live.

But why can we trust God for the best life?

First, Honda's engineers made the bike and know it best. God made the world and knows it best. When we change the design, we end up like Joe's bike. And that's exactly what we do. Often. We explain away God's rules, because we think we know better. Yes, connecting with a local church is normative, but Sunday is our only day to sleep in. We don't have to go to church to know Jesus. Yes, sexual intercourse should be within marriage, but times have changed. Sex, like any appetite, should be satisfied in a way that brings the most pleasure. Yes, God wants our words to be "with gentleness and respect" (1 Peter 3:15), but we feel so much passion about our favorite political candidate.

The list goes on and on as we plug in our excuses. But when we do this, we proclaim that we know better than God.

Second, just as Honda wants to provide a good ride, God wants to bless and enrich our lives. Jesus said, "My purpose is to give them a rich and satisfying life" (John 10:10 NLT). Other translations use the word "abundant." Honestly, until we get this, we'll always struggle with the rules. Think of God's Word as the operator's manual of life, written by the Designer to benefit the user. So when we follow, we benefit. Why would God give arbitrary commands that have no purpose behind them? I remember a schoolteacher like that, and I thought of him as an uncaring tyrant.

Third, remember that not only does God know best and tell us how to find the best life, but he does it all out of abundant love, "This is how much God loved the world: He gave his Son, his one and only Son. And this is why: so that no one need be destroyed; by believing in him, anyone can have a whole and lasting life" (John 3:16 MSG). That love underlies all he does for us, every command.

Frankly, I'm still working on all this, but I'm growing. Recently I reflected on how satisfying my life is now, particularly compared to my earlier trajectory. Following Jesus is the biggest no-brainer of all time. And my worst times have been when I thought I was smarter than God. He's God. I'm not. And I live better with that.

KICK-STARTING THE DISCUSSION

Have you thought of God's rules as a source of loss? How? Which ones? Why? Have you seen the benefits of following God's lifestyle? Can you think of a time when following a rule seemed stupid, but you did and benefitted? What one command of God can you obey this week?

18

BE YOURSELF

Create, Don't Copy, Your Riding Style

Ever notice how you can fairly consistently identify a rider's bike by his gear? Spot a dude with a lot of black leather, maybe a denim vest with a patch of some kind, a half helmet, engineer boots. Odds are he rides a Harley. Especially if he's middle-aged. But if he wears multicolored leather or Cordura with armor, a full-face helmet, look for a crotch-rocket sport bike.

If he has gray hair, jeans, a ratty T-shirt, and maybe cowboy boots, look for a vintage model of some brand. Should he be wearing a three-piece suit and tie, you'll likely find a Honda Gold Wing close by. Okay, the last is an exaggeration. And really, all of these examples extend the truth a bit.

We do tend to follow trends and friends. A neighbor who is from Germany understandably rode BMWs for years, until all his friends had Japanese crotch rockets. Pretty soon he rode one too. And it seems like most guys who begin riding in their middle years, after the kids have left the nest, ride Harleys. We follow trends. We try to fit in.

But to maximize the benefits of riding, we need to know ourselves: the type of riding we most enjoy—around town or the twisties or longer tours; our love of speed—a lot of it or to just relax; our preference for cornering—scraping our pegs or barely leaning. No one combo is right for all, so figure out how you want to ride, then decide what you'll ride. Just don't mindlessly copy the trends or your friends.

Following Jesus follows that pattern. We have a lot of options on how to do it. And just as with riding, some absolutes exist, like gravity, centripetal force, and balance. Following Jesus also comes with some nonnegotiables that transcend our choices.

Absolutes of Following

A friend and theologian, Scott Bartchy, uses a grid that guides us in knowing what's central for us. Normative passages reveal the normal Christian life by commands God has given. They rank at the top of authority. Descriptive passages carry less weight and tell the narrative of what happened, but with no command attached. Problematic passages apply a specific principle to a specific issue and rank at the bottom.

A passage from Ephesians lists seven traits that unite Christians. Perhaps we can safely classify them as key absolutes: "Make every effort to keep the unity of the Spirit through the bond of peace. There is *one body* and *one Spirit*, just as you were called to *one hope* when you were called, *one Lord, one faith, one baptism; one God* and Father of all, who is over all and through all and in all" (Ephesians 4:3-6).

To summarize, God unites us by the person and nature of the one God in the persons of the Father, the Son, and the Spirit; by the body of Christ, which is the church; by the one hope of eternal life; by the one faith in Jesus that transforms our lives; by the one baptism signifying our entry into a relationship with God.

These are key traits we all should have. But apart from these seven comes great flexibility in crafting our spiritual lives.

Freedom of Following

Early on, the first-century church struggled with freedom, as many thought all Christians should share the same beliefs on all issues.

The early church had vegans and carnivores, Saturday worshippers and Sunday ones, those who drank alcohol and those who did not. Granted, they agreed on the absolutes, but they thought agreement should extend further. Kind of like thinking all bikers should choose our ride.

That merely led to judging and division, which Paul addressed pretty clearly.

> Accept other believers who are weak in faith, and don't argue with them about what they think is right or wrong. For instance, one person believes it's all right to eat anything. But another believer with a sensitive conscience will eat only vegetables. Those who feel free to eat anything must not look down on those who don't. And those who don't eat certain foods must not condemn those who do, for God has accepted them (Romans 14:1-3 NLT).

God granted us great freedom with an importance that far transcends choosing a Harley or Honda or Ducati or Victory. What makes us think we can require behavior that God himself chose never to require?

We may prefer a liturgical or informal worship service—both are good. We may prefer Saturday over Sunday worship—both are good. We may choose to drink alcohol in moderation or abstain—both are good. We may choose to not use the charismatic gifts or use them—both are good. The list continues, but we need to see the importance and breadth of granting others the right to their own opinion without looking down on them. And we ask them to respect our opinions as well.

All riders share a unique fellowship regardless of their ride and their gear. All followers of Jesus have a unique fellowship despite their individual choices about how they follow him. Let's give ourselves the freedom to choose our style of riding or following.

And just as we figure out the kind of riding we enjoy and getting a bike based on that, get to know yourself spiritually. Your strengths and weaknesses, your joys and bummers, your experiences and successes and failures. Spend some time evaluating your choices. Ask trusted friends for their thoughts.

Then craft your life like you craft your riding. Match your choices with the person God created you to be. Don't copy anyone else; that's suicide to the real you.

KICK-STARTING THE APPLICATION

How much pressure do you feel to go along with others? Do you often feel you violate your personhood when you do? How can you better craft a clear and accurate take on the real you? How can God help you carry that out?

19

GO ALONG

The Joy of Riding Together

Although part of my nature includes being a lone wolf, biking has taught me the importance of connections, of not just traveling together on bikes but through life. Jerry, Rich, and I began riding together in our early 20s, when we all had hair and carried fewer pounds. That friendship has added Mick and Brad and has grown into the Gray Hogs—gray representing what hair we still have, hogs from our love of food.

So far we've hit 20 states and 2 countries with no plans to stop, in part because the advantages of riding together continue to teach me what I need to know about life. On one trip, the damp chill that comes off the Pacific along the Olympic Peninsula penetrated our bones, and we welcomed the end of day at a hotel at Lake Quinault. We showered, had a nice meal, and sat on the porch overlooking the lake as the sun drove away the clouds.

But our companionship had more value than even the warmth we found at the end of the day. We told stories about the day's ride. We complained about who felt the coldest. We ragged on the guy who lagged farthest behind the group. That togetherness brought another benefit in Libby, Montana. Mick loves to find new roads, and at breakfast one morning he brought along a grin and a map. "Hey, guys, look at this road. It cuts off the route we planned to take here. Look at the curves, and it's marked scenic. Wanna give it a shot?"

We did, and we found some roads we never would have found, except for our companion who lived to find new territory.

Once in Oregon, heading from Salem to Mount St. Helens, Jerry invited two riders from his church—Rick and Renita—to join us. They took us on a tour of every back road, some that most maps likely ignored, and we experienced parts of Oregon we would never have found without some locals leading the way. They rode with us for the day, and then when they learned we were going farther north, they donated some rain pants to keep us a little drier.

Keep in mind, riding together is cheaper because two can share the cost of a motel room. It took a page to begin to list some of the benefits of riding together, but let's get to the spiritual lesson.

God designed his followers to travel together through life. I can't find a single example in the New Testament of a solo Christian not involved with a local fellowship. But George Barna's studies suggest that while 73% of Americans self-identify as Christians, only 31% qualify as active Christians: those who self-identify, who attend worship just once a month, and say faith is important to them. Or, 42% have little or no connection with other believers in a local church.[1] So why do we travel together?

We Obey Together

You can't be a rider if you don't own or have access to a bike and ride. That's the concept, right? So how does God conceive of followers? He commands that we connect regularly with a group of fellow believers: "[Do] not give up meeting together, as some are in the habit of doing" (Hebrews 10:25). Of the 22 New Testament letters, 8 were for all believers, 2 went to individuals, and 12 were to churches or their pastors. Church sounds important. No churches, and we'd lose almost half of the New Testament.

God also describes the church as the body of Jesus, with each follower a different member: "All of you together are Christ's body, and each of you is a part of it" (1 Corinthians 12:27 NLT). If my right hand becomes separated from my body, not only will it make riding tough, but that hand will wither and die. The word for *church* in the original language means "to assemble." If we all are the body of Christ, do we assemble with the rest of our body?

We Worship Together

Riders share a common passion, namely, riding. Followers share a common passion, namely, God. Some of my most awesome times of worship have come when I'm alone. Yes, I can worship at a trout stream or on a bike. But alone I can't match what occurs in corporate worship. Let's change the metaphor to body surfing, where you get caught up in the power of what surrounds you, jump on, and get carried faster than you ever could on your own.

That's corporate worship, sharing our common adoration for God and getting moved. A lot of New Testament books mention weekly gatherings, but this is one of the best: "On the first day of the week, we gathered with the local believers to share in the Lord's Supper. Paul was preaching" (Acts 20:7 NLT).

We Serve Together

Riding together allows us to do far more than we can alone, as does connecting with a local body of believers. Ever hear of an atheist's hospital? Orphanage? Homeless ministry? Didn't think so. But coming together, working together, we accomplish far more than going it alone.

Sure, some tasks are solo. I get that. But when Jesus sent out his followers as the first missionaries, they went two together (Mark 6:7).

After the Day of Pentecost, the start of the church, over 3,000 people accepted Christ. That group went out and changed the world. Serving together.

We Connect Together

One of the greatest joys of our group trips comes from companionship. Sharing stories. Helping. Notice the reason behind the believers meeting together: "Let us consider how we may spur one another on toward love and good deeds, not giving up meeting together, as some are in the habit of doing, but encouraging one another" (Hebrews 10:24-25). We Gray Hogs trust each other because we've spent a lot of time together. Several of the hogs have told me of areas in which I need to grow. That's a nice spur. And followers, when connected, help each other to grow. But without spending significant time with other people, we have little impact on them and vice versa.

KICK-STARTING THE APPLICATION

How committed are you to a local group of believers? Is the connection enough to benefit you in the four dimensions above? Do you think God would have you more involved? How? If you need to improve, what will you do this week?

20

GO ALONE

The Joy of Riding Solo

Okay, I know our last chapter said we should go together (and we should), but we also need to go alone sometimes. As much as I love riding with the Gray Hogs, a solo trip when I was 26 changed my life. After a month-long mission trip to the Taos, New Mexico, area ended in '74, I loaded a duffle and sleeping bag on my 750 Honda and took off in search of America. Solo. My destination was wherever I ended up.

Before running out of money and nice weather, I'd traveled 13,000 miles, hit 31 states, and met a lot of new friends. I must have visited every historic site and museum along the way, and I took a lot of side roads with no idea of where they headed.

And I found out a lot about both America and myself. I had myriad experiences on that solo trip. Here are a few benefits of going alone.

Freedom

Human nature yearns for freedom—that is, the ability to do. To choose. Solo riding put me on roads the Gray Hogs have never attempted, from asphalt interstates to blue lines on a map to gravel to dirt. On my rides with the hogs, we visited only one museum, and that was because a storm in Coos Bay socked us in. Compare that to dozens of museum visits when I was on a solo trip.

Our group ride once took a quick walk through the Independence Ghost Town outside Aspen. But on my own, I spent days exploring Colonial Williamsburg. Which is better? Neither. And while I appreciate the group decisions on route choices, I also enjoyed making those solo decisions, to head where I wanted to go. Group trips don't allow me a chance to wet a fishing line, yet my solo rides provided more than one meal of fresh trout.

Spiritual freedom carries more value. "You will know the truth, and the truth will set you free…Everyone who sins is a slave to sin…So if the Son sets you free, you will be free indeed" (John 8:32,34,36). Coming to Jesus lets us consistently resist the domination of sin. Yeah, we'll still sin, but spiritual freedom allows us to say no. We have the freedom to maximize who we can become. To overcome past mistakes and abuse.

Even more, following Jesus becomes a dance, balancing the leading of Jesus with the freedom he gives. Every time I've seen the Bible say something is God's will for you, period, it deals with either salvation or sanctification. God wants us to know him. To become like him in character and mission.

Beyond that we have great freedom. To craft our lives within those two boundaries from above. Paul gives a great example of choice: "When I went to Troas to preach the gospel of Christ and found that the Lord had opened a door for me, I still had no peace of mind, because I did not find my brother Titus there. So I said goodbye to them and went on to Macedonia. But thanks be to God, who always leads us in triumphal procession in Christ" (2 Corinthians 2:12-14).

Simplicity

When I taught at a Christian junior high, finances were tight, and to save on motel bills when riding, I usually looked for a safe place to throw down a sleeping bag. Campgrounds, rest areas, or places out of sight. Yeah, that led to some problems whenever rain exploded from above, so I had to occasionally get a room.

But now two of the Gray Hogs carry CPAP machines (and they need electricity), and we all appreciate hot showers at the end of a day's ride. Rides today don't share the simplicity of my earlier days.

Keeping it simple allowed me to travel farther and see much more than a more luxurious trip normally allows. And I learned something about the necessities of life. We can live more simply than we imagine or often desire.

I want to spark some thoughts here and not proclaim them as essentials. But ponder this: Could we have more ministry opportunities if our mortgages weren't so much? If we reduced our debt? If we gave up overtime or a second job in order to spend more time with family, friends, and church? If we gave up some of our toys and exchanged the resources and time to invest more in people?

I'm guilty here. My wife and I own four vehicles. A Honda for the family car, a Mustang convertible for fun, an F150 pickup for camping and hauling, and my Honda ST1300. I find it hard to justify having four, so the Mustang is on the way out.

The goal isn't to guilt anyone but to encourage all of us to evaluate how simplifying our lives might open up some spiritual opportunities.

Interactions with Decent Folks

Solo riding on a bike provides opportunities for great interactions. When riding in a group, we tend to focus on our fellow riders. But when I'm alone, I've found a lot of people to talk to. On one trip, I had a couple of problems with people, and both were law enforcement officers determined to hassle a guy on a bike. Both times, two other cops made the situations right.

The overall decency of my fellow Americans struck me. One solo ride occurred during the time of the Watergate scandal, near the end of the Vietnam War, and skepticism abounded across the country. But several strangers invited me to spend a night at their house. Another biker invited me to share his site when a campground was full. The trip changed my perceptions of people.

Decency doesn't mean they followed Jesus, or that they'd achieved the perfection I still strive for. But it helped me understand a bit of why God loves all people. It's caused me to change how I initially approach people—with less suspicion and giving them the benefit of the doubt. To see them as people created by God and why he said, "That's very good," right after.

KICK-STARTING THE APPLICATION

What do you like most about solo and group rides? How can you better use the spiritual freedom that following Jesus brings? How can you increase the simplicity in your life? What do you see as the benefits? Do you see people as basically decent? Does your view of people reflect God's love for them?

21

AN OPEN MIND ON THE OPEN ROAD

Not Knowing Can Cost You

Our 2017 destination was Banff, Canada. The weather forecast was rain. All over. We rode east through Washington, skirting the Canadian border. Mick's bucket list included Banff, but the weather to the north was colder and wetter than what we were experiencing on this side of the border—at least until we hit Sandpoint, Idaho. The rain came down heavier and the temperature dropped even more. We sheltered in place at a motel, trying to wait it out. Days passed.

When a brief window of blue sky opened, the desk clerk recommended a route north along Kootenay Lake in Canada, even though Banff continued to get drenched farther to the north. Since we needed to ride, we headed north in the damp chill. A free ferry (standard in Canada), took us across the lake, and as soon as we parked the bikes, Jerry and I headed to a snack bar for some hot drinks. I ordered a pastry and coffee for $5. When I reached for my wallet, I found I'd left it locked in the bike.

So I asked Jerry to loan me the 5 dollars, but he only had a $20 bill, which he gave me. I gave that to the clerk, and she handed my change back—a $20 Canadian bill. I had thought everyone would take American dollars. They did. And they exchanged it for a Canadian bill. A Canadian $20 bill, worth about $15 US. That bill resided in my dresser drawer for a year until we finally hit Banff the next year, where I waved it in Jerry's face and paid a bill with it. But for a year, that coffee and pastry cost me $20 US—and that exchange also wrote this chapter.

Since our return, I've learned that US currency is an inconvenience in Canadian stores. They have to exchange it, and many Canadians view the use of US currency in the Great White North as disrespectful to them. It's kind of like a Mexican using pesos in California to pay for things. I understand now. I just should have known it before the trip! When we travel or connect with another subculture, we need to know their customs and laws. One hand gesture understood as positive in America is vulgar in some other societies. And crossing your legs and revealing the bottom of your shoe is a huge insult in others.

In following Jesus, we need the same knowledge and sensitivity to those with different backgrounds. We all interact with people beyond our comfort zones.

Know the Cultures

Culture isn't primarily ethnicity but (according to Merriam-Webster) the "customary beliefs, social forms, and material traits" of a group. Their way of life. Their traits. And groups can vary from one nation to another or even subcultures in the same nation. Followers and nonfollowers have different cultures, as do denominations and local churches and political parties. Regions maintain differences. The Bible Belt won't match the Pacific Northwest in many ways. And if we desire to impact them all for Jesus, we need to be aware of these differences.

Paul used his knowledge of other cultures, particularly when addressing a crowd in Athens:

> People of Athens! I see that in every way you are very religious. For as I walked around and looked carefully at your objects of worship, I even found an altar with this inscription: TO AN UNKNOWN GOD. So you are ignorant of the very thing you worship—and this is what I am going to proclaim to you (Acts 17:22-23).

He began with their beliefs and used that as a jumping-off point. He even quoted their own literature to them to support his position: "As some of your own poets have said, 'We are his offspring.' Therefore since we are God's offspring, we should not..." (verses 28-29).

Maybe we can follow that pattern. We don't need to approve of another's positions, but unless they know we will listen to them, that we know their true position, we have little chance of developing either a good conversation or relationship. So we listen. We ask genuine questions, not gotchas. We try to discover why they believe as they do.

But more than just knowing, we need to adapt to them. Not to blindly accept, but to fit in when we can without betraying biblical principles. The classic line can help us: People won't care how much you know, until they know how much you care.

Adapt to Cultures

Paul worked in three cultures: the Jewish one in which he grew up, the Greek culture that valued philosophy, and the Roman culture that embraced structure. And more than just knowing their distinctives, he adapted when he could.

> To the Jews I *became like a Jew*, to win the Jews. To those under the law I *became like one under the law* (though I myself am not under the law), so as to win those under

the law. To those not having the law I *became like one not having the law* (though I am not free from God's law but am under Christ's law), so as to win those not having the law. To the weak I became weak, to win the weak. I have become all things to all people so that by all possible means I might save some (1 Corinthians 9:20-22).

Truly, we walk a narrow line as we adapt to the cultures of those around us. We live in the world and fit into it in some ways and remain countercultural in others. But to the level we can, let's identify with unbelievers, learn their values and language, and strive to understand when we cannot agree. Why? So, like Paul, we might save some.

KICK-STARTING THE APPLICATION

How much interaction do you have with members of other groups? Does that make God smile? How knowledgeable are you of those groups? Would they say you understand their values and customs? What do you suspect God would respond to your answers? How can you improve this week?

22

EXPECT DANGER

Some People Are Just Bad...Know That

Scenes from the event remain fresh despite the passing of more than 40 years. Our church fellowship had a huge gathering each summer at Newport Dunes, featuring too much sun for this then-blond guy, a lot of activities, and an evening service with music and a message. I rode there on my Honda 350 from my home in Long Beach, and Ken asked for a ride back.

At a light in Seal Beach, the bike stalled, short on gas, just as the light turned green. I quickly turned the valve for the gas reserve and restarted the engine right away, maybe taking five seconds. But that exhausted the patience of the car driver behind me. Honking and then tailgating. The bike's maneuverability kept me safe, but the aggressive driver continued to chase me while I looked for a cop. No luck. Finally, the driver dropped out of sight, and a few miles later I turned into a gas station on Bellflower Boulevard to tank up.

When I pulled back onto the street, the driver returned and moved in behind me again—close. Apparently, he'd spotted me at the station and waited. In ambush. So the chase resumed. We approached the apartment complex where Ken lived with his folks, and I made a quick left turn the car couldn't follow, and I turned down an alley to

94

the back entrance to Ken's apartment. Ken jumped off the bike and I jumped on the gas, only to see the car turn down the alley. Right in front of me. Maybe 100 feet away. Moving toward me.

Until then I'd never realized how nimbly my bike could make a U-turn. Heart racing and without Ken on the back, I lost the driver pretty fast after a few more turns. And I'd discovered something about some people.

Some just love doing wrong. Because of five seconds at a light, this driver gave up half an hour to try to run me over. I had no doubts about his intention. Still don't. Just one example: We need to recognize the reality of evil.

No Judging?

We live in an age that celebrates "no judging." Even in the Christian community. Even in the moral realm. But this is yesterday's news. The theme of the Old Testament book of Judges is about judging: "In those days Israel had no king [political and spiritual leadership]; everyone did as they saw fit" (Judges 17:6; see also 18:1, 19:1, 21:25). We hesitate to make moral judgments because our culture has no commonly accepted spiritual value base.

But living in a world with evil requires that we judge or be bulldozed. If I had assumed the car driver was really a good guy at heart, I'd have been run over and likely would never have been able to write this chapter.

Evil Exists

An awareness of the reality of evil allows us to live in the real world. According to Jesus: "A good man brings good things out of the good stored up in his heart, and an evil man brings evil things out of the evil stored up in his heart" (Luke 6:45). Some people are evil. Period. And even good people do evil things. We call that sin.

Most people are basically decent and helpful. But some allow evil to reign in their lives. And for us to follow Jesus, we need to distinguish between good and evil. That requires judging.

Judging Now

In this life God tells us to make a number of judgments. Paul gave the most extensive instructions: "Test everything...Hold on to what is good. Stay away from every kind of evil" (1 Thessalonians 5:21-22). That's judging, and every aspect of our lives with a moral component needs testing to see if it leads to God or to Satan.

We also judge our fellow believers to see if they're trustworthy, reliable, and have leadership capabilities: "What business is it of mine to judge those outside the church? Are you not to judge those inside?" (1 Corinthians 5:12). Paul also tells us to help each other in dealing with sin: "Brothers and sisters, if someone is caught in a sin, you who live by the Spirit should restore that person gently" (Galatians 6:1). Doesn't that require judging if an act constitutes sin?

Judging also applies to ourselves: "If we were more discerning with regard to ourselves, we would not come under such judgment" (1 Corinthians 11:31). I like this verse. If I examine my own actions and motives, I need not fear genuine judgment from God or my fellow Christians.

But in doing this, we need grace to guide our every step: "Do not judge others, and you will not be judged. For you will be treated as you treat others. The standard you use in judging is the standard by which you will be judged" (Matthew 7:1-2 NLT). Yes, we judge. But Jesus suggests that if we desire to be judged with grace and mercy and understanding, then we should include those qualities as we judge. Hmm.

Judging Later

These two examples boggle my mind. Notice the future tense here: "Don't you realize that someday we believers will judge the world? And since you are going to judge the world, can't you decide even these little things among yourselves?" (1 Corinthians 6:2 NLT). We'll play a role in God's final judgment.

But the next verse takes judging to a deeper level: "Don't you realize that we will judge angels? So you should surely be able to resolve ordinary disputes in this life" (verse 3 NLT). I have no clue what this means! But it certainly enhances the fact that we do judge.

Judging Never

But we need to avoid some judging, particularly when we become rigid and harsh: "Judgment without mercy will be shown to anyone who has not been merciful. Mercy triumphs over judgment" (James 2:13). We call this judgmentalism, an attitude that turns the world off.

Also, let's let Jesus be God, the one judging the eternal destiny of people: "When the Son of Man comes in his glory, and all the angels with him, he will sit on his glorious throne. All the nations will be gathered before him, and he will separate the people...They will go away into eternal punishment, but the righteous will go to eternal life" (Matthew 25:31,46).

So do we judge? Yep. We must to identify wrong and avoid it. But may mercy and grace go along.

KICK-STARTING THE APPLICATION

What is your basis of moral absolutes? Your view of judging? How often do you make intentional judgments about good and evil? How well do you combine mercy and grace with your judging?

23

BE A BOY SCOUT: PREPARE

Riding Has Dangers, So Does Life

Heading home from our first cross-country ride to Kansas, Sheila and I pulled the Gold Wing into Durango just as the rain hit. Heavy. We found a café to wait it out, saw a break in the weather, and made a dash for Flagstaff. Not many miles passed before dark storm clouds formed ahead and then dropped on us. We took a quick pause to put on our rain gear, and ten miles later the skies cleared.

We took another quick stop to change. About 15 miles later the rain clouds formed once more, the rain came down, and then another pause. Honestly, we stopped at least eight times to gear up or gear down, and we appreciated remaining mostly dry. This was Sheila's first long ride, and she received a good lesson on preparing for problems.

The joy of riding is balanced by the dangers and problems and inconveniences. They abound. So we prepare for them. Rain gear. Cold gear. Good tires. A first-aid kit. Coffee cups. And a lot more.

Likewise, the spiritual life comes with dangers. Some because life has problems. Some because we all make mistakes and consequences follow. Some from temptations and spiritual attacks from Satan. Jesus knew that well, and he promised: "Here on earth you will have many trials and sorrows" (John 16:33 NLT). And the biking life provides some great lessons in crafting good spiritual gear for the dangers and difficulties ahead.

Awareness

In my early days, an experienced biker suggested looking at every car as being intentionally out to get me. Wise advice that's become a habit. But the greatest danger comes not from them but us. Researchers at Virginia Tech studied motorcycle crashes by putting cameras on 100 riders of all ages. They rode a total of more than 360,000 miles. They chronicled 99 events with another vehicle: 19 times the other vehicle was at fault, and 35 times the biker collided with the other vehicle. Add aggressive driving and inattention, and the risk increased 30-fold.[1] So we have to look out for others *and* we have to look out for ourselves.

Following Jesus matches that. My greatest danger is focusing so much on the material world that I ignore the spiritual one. And that spiritual world comes with greater dangers than the material one, according to the apostle Peter: "Stay alert! Watch out for your great enemy, the devil. He prowls around like a roaring lion, looking for someone to devour" (1 Peter 5:8 NLT).

In *My Utmost for His Highest,* Oswald Chambers wrote, "An unguarded strength is a double weakness."[2] Even if we have strength in a particular area, if we don't pay attention, we can be vulnerable. So, on a bike, look for issues that might bring damage. And when following Jesus, maintain an awareness of an enemy who wants more than to just cause us to drop our bike.

When a situation arises with a possible spiritual significance, think and pray about it. What are the consequences? What would God most desire?

Responsibility

Face it. Every time we ride, our lives are on the line. When I didn't check the quality of my rear tire and went down, the tire manufacturer didn't go down. I did. When going through a canyon outside Deadwood, South Dakota, right at the limit of balance, I chose to wave at a passing biker even though it influenced the delicate balance of my bike on the roadway. I made that choice; he didn't make it for me. Statistically, if there's a collision with another vehicle, the chances are two-to-one the biker made the mistake, according to the Virginia Tech study. Blaming others doesn't work because it's likely we're the ones who have to pay the price.

In following Jesus, it's our lives on the line. Yes, others have wounded and abused and taken advantage of us. But we own our responses. We choose how we respond. A pastor suggested we all have an age (he suggested around 25) when we need to quit blaming others and realize we're the person we chose to become.

When we stand before God's throne, he looks at what we've done. First, did we accept Jesus as Savior and Lord? Second, how did we serve him? Our best? Just average? That decision, according to Paul, has eternal consequences:

> No one can lay any foundation other than the one already laid, which is Jesus Christ. If anyone builds on this foundation using gold, silver, costly stones, wood, hay or straw, their work will be shown for what it is, because the Day will bring it to light... The fire will test the quality of each person's work. If what he has built survives, the builder will receive a reward. If it is burned up, the builder will suffer loss but yet will be saved—even though only as one escaping through the flames (1 Corinthians 3:11-15).

So as we navigate the open road of following Jesus, let's realize that our choices count. For eternity. No excuses.

Skill

Just one month after I started riding bikes, I headed to Canada on a Honda 350 Scrambler—and that might qualify as one of my most idiotic choices ever. I didn't know enough about riding to navigate the dangers. A friend accurately described me as "one of nature's babes." That Virginia Tech study on bike accidents concluded that a lack of skill and experience caused a significant increase in accidents. Now, after 40 years of riding, not many roads and routes scare me. But it took many miles to get me to this point.

Growth in Christ adds more good gear to our walk with Jesus. We've seen the hidden dangers of temptation. We've gotten to know the owner's guide better and that it works. We've moved beyond the emotions of the beginning to a settled maturity, and we are in the process: "Like newborn babies, you must crave pure spiritual milk so that you will grow into a full experience of salvation. Cry out for this nourishment" (1 Peter 2:2 NLT).

If we do it right, if we rely on good spiritual gear, then we continually get closer to the person God designed us to be.

KICK-STARTING THE APPLICATION

How often do you think of the dangers of riding and following Jesus? Of the three types of gear mentioned, which is your strongest? Which is your weakest, needing growth? Why? How can you develop that one?

24

EXPLORE ALL OPTIONS

Life Requires a Lot of Flexing

Back in '78 I headed to a local Honda dealership to get an oil filter for my '73 750. A salesman strolled over with a deal I couldn't refuse, and I rode out on a nearly new '78 Gold Wing. Thirty-three years and 70,000 miles later, the Gray Hogs headed into Deadwood, South Dakota, and the Gold Wing began to run rough and exhaust a foul-smelling smoke.

We straggled into town, booked some rooms, and I worked on the bike a bit. No luck. The next day we limped into the nearest town, Sturgis, and, long story short, I left the Wing behind and rode out on a 2009 Kawasaki Vulcan 900 LT. The trouble came when I was back home in SoCal and trying to register the bike at our AAA office.

Because the bike was less than two years old, California's Department of Motor Vehicles assumed I'd attempted to avoid paying the state sales tax, so their regulations wouldn't allow it. Just a bit frustrated, I'd paid thousands of dollars for a bike I couldn't legally ride.

I said as much to the clerk, and he said, "Wait a minute. I have an idea." Pulling out a huge book, at least four inches thick, he went over dozens of sections and then smiled. "So your vehicle broke down out of state, and this vehicle replaced your old bike? We're golden. That's an exception." After I paid a small transfer fee, I rode back home with a smile.

I learned that sometimes our goals get frustrated and we need to examine our options. Sometimes a lot of them. My first goal was to ride the Wing home. No go. The next, to find a new bike. A go, but I had to check out several dealers. Then I had to register it. No go at first. Only after a lot of research to find an exception did everything work out.

Thus I'd found another bike-inspired lesson for following Jesus.

Grab a Goal

Every bike trip includes some form of destination, and looking ahead to our spiritual future fits within God's plans: "If they had any sense at all, they'd know this; they would see what's coming down the road" (Deuteronomy 32:29 MSG). What plans do we have for our spiritual open road? On the big goals list, heaven should top it. Growing closer to Jesus and becoming more Christlike should follow.

But we need some smaller, more specific goals also. How will we serve God? When and how should we adapt those? What steps will we take to grow? To connect with others? What careers fit us best?

God wants us to look to the future, but he includes a caution: "Since no man knows the future, who can tell someone else what is to come?" (Ecclesiastes 8:7). So we hold a loose grip on our goals. Well, the specific ones. Keep the generals. Several goals on that Deadwood trip were thwarted. When I was leaving Long Beach, I had no clue the future included coming home on another bike. But once we have some goals, we take the next step.

Start a Strategy

Once we know our destination, we start to choose our route, both with bikes and with God: "In his heart humans plan their course, but the LORD determines their steps" (Proverbs 16:9). We get specific in planning how to reach our goal. Yet we hold those plans loosely, because God often changes them.

In a recent message, pastor Steve Redden covered four ways God answers our prayers: delivered, denied, delayed, or different. Looking back, I thought of many specific prayers God hadn't delivered as I wanted but ended up being answers I now rejoice in.

I can accept that, because I'm convinced God operates in the realm of love. He cares for us enough to let his Son take on humanity and guilt and sin for us. So when he says later or no, I trust his motivation.

And he knows best. He knows our strengths and weaknesses and potential. He knows our friends and family and associates. He knows the future much better than we do. And he does that with every individual on earth. He also knows his plans for the human race and our world. Somehow he combines all that in a manner I can't begin to imagine. At a conference, author Keith Miller said that knowing two truths will get us through life. One, God is real. Two, we're not him. That helps us in the next step.

Avoid Arrogance

Sometimes, not often, but sometimes, we get a bit full of ourselves. We've done well. Life slides smoothly along. And we know what should come next. That arrogance can bite us in the rump: "Now listen, you who say, 'Today or tomorrow we will go to this or that city, spend a year there, carry on business and make money.' Why, you do not even know what will happen tomorrow. What is your life? You are a mist that appears for a little while and then vanishes. Instead, you ought to say, 'If it is the Lord's will, we will live and do this or that.' As it is, you boast and brag. All such boasting is evil" (James 4:13-16).

Tennessee Ernie Ford often used the classic line, "The good Lord willin' and the creek don't rise." I like that and try to use it often. It keeps me humble, because so much of my life exceeds my control. Creeks rise. Friends betray. Economies crash. Jobs end. Spouses leave.

Yes, let's grab some goals. Let's start strategies to reach them. And in both, let's explore all the options available, gather all the information, and then humbly say, "God, if it's okay with you, I'd like to…"

KICK-STARTING THE APPLICATION

What are some of your key goals for life? What is your strategy to reach them? How did you gather information and options? How did you involve God in the process? Think of a time when a plan fell apart. How did you respond? Do you typically hold onto plans tightly or more loosely? What does that say about your faith? How can you weave God more into the process?

25

SHARE THE JOY

Extend the Joy of Riding to Others

For six years we lived in Thousand Oaks, and one Easter weekend our kids, who lived 130 miles away in Fallbrook, drove up with our two grandkids. Yeah, the house was a bit crowded. For the Easter feast, we planned on a restaurant in nearby Camarillo, and I offered our daughter, Teri, and our granddaughter, Hannah, a ride there on the bike. One going, the other returning. Hannah jumped on it.

We geared her up with jeans, boots, a light jacket, and a helmet. And while the others took a car on the freeway, we headed down a back road on a narrow, twisty canyon to the Oxnard plain and then cruised through some farm fields and narrow country roads. She proved to be a natural biker, leaning just right from the first turn. A grin covered her face upon our arrival at the restaurant.

After lunch I told Teri it was her turn, but Hannah interjected, "Mom, please, can I ride back too?" The loving mom yielded, Hannah again hopped on, and we traveled a number of fresh roads before heading up the canyon.

Yeah, they arrived before we did, but we had more fun. They met us outside. Her sacrificial mom asked about the ride, and Hannah said, beaming, "This was the best day of my life!"

A natural biker girl and a very happy biker granddad. I enjoyed her joy, and that sparked some pondering. In our current world, with all the political disagreement and partisanship, with many struggling financially, with homelessness at a peak, with the opioid crisis and more, perhaps we followers should commit to increasing the joy in the world. And act intentionally. I have two tips on doing that.

A Spirit of Generosity

Most of us struggle with selfishness. We look out for number one despite knowing the identity of the One. We deserve a break today. Yes, we blend selfishness with selflessness, but too often the former wins. At least with me. And when we all look out primarily for ourselves, life becomes a battle. Survival of the fittest. We find ourselves pitted against one another, and we only get happiness whenever we win over someone else. That happiness soon ends, and little joy endures after our petty battles.

What if we flipped the scenario? We can still take care of our needs, but we can also choose to care for others? Doesn't God tell us to do that? "*Not looking to only your own interests* but each of you [should look] *to the interests of the others*" (Philippians 2:4). If we take no care for ourselves, we can't help others. If we only take care of ourselves, we won't help others.

Frankly, giving Hannah a ride on the bike wouldn't count as a sacrifice. But I added some joy to her life. That seems like a good act. But let's transcend bike riding. Let's build generosity into our actions and our character: "You will be made enriched *in every way* so that you can be generous *on every occasion*, and through us your generosity will result in thanksgiving to God" (2 Corinthians 9:11). I really struggle with this.

My struggle comes in part from an innate selfishness. I own that. But we need to realize generosity transcends finances. Note the phrase "in every way."

Andy, our home group leader and a dentist, knows an optometrist in town who's worked in the same building for 27 years. A nearby dry cleaner tainted the premises, forcing the optometrist to move. Overwhelmed with all the work, he asked his synagogue to help and received—nothing. Then Andy asked if our group would help him pack. Even so, a lot was left to be done, and he needed to be out the next day. So three of us retired old guys spent five hours the next day working on the move. Andy and his wife helped his friend more that night. Everything was moved. And he came to our home group the next week. A lot of thanksgiving was directed to God for a generous use of time and health.

What if we looked for opportunities like this to bless other people? To do what we can rather than rationalize that we're too busy, we have stuff to do, we need to rest and take care of ourselves. Yes, we take care of our needs. But let's exhibit generosity in any way we can. I suspect that would impact people significantly.

A Spirit of Inner Joy

We can go beyond the acts to our attitudes. Think for a moment of the tone found too frequently on social media, where personal insults dominate disagreements. Where vile language abounds. Where some seem to post only complaints and criticisms. My question to myself and to each of you is this: Does the tone of our lives express joy or do we look like professional lemon suckers?

Knowing God should result in a joy that fills our spirit regardless of the external conditions: "You have made known to me the paths of life; you will *fill me with joy* in your presence" (Acts 2:28). Does that match our reality? God gives this joy merely by his presence in our lives. It's a sovereign gift to us. But do we receive it? Do we nurture it?

It actually needs nurturing. Paul commanded: "*Always be full of joy* in the Lord. I say it again—rejoice…Don't worry about anything; instead, pray about everything" (Philippians 4:4,6 NLT).

Think with me a bit. If we recognize God's presence in our lives, if we intentionally choose to cultivate joy as our default attitude, if we avoid worry by taking all our needs and problems and concerns to him, then won't we change? Won't that transform our words? Our interactions? Our demeanor?

Shouldn't our faces shine like Hannah's after riding with Grandpa? And shouldn't that bring joy to others?

KICK-STARTING THE APPLICATION

Would your friends say that joy dominates your life? What most keeps you from having joy? How well do you pass joy along to others? How can you do more?

26

BORN TO BE WILD, LIVING MILD

Balancing Adventure and Responsibility

Before each road trip on the bike, I play Steppenwolf's "Born to be Wild." Loud. Quite loud as I fire up the motor and head for the highway. My soul needs adventure. A challenge to test myself, to move beyond my fears. Riding particularly comes with risks, but few choices match the selfishness that adventure seeking can bring.

As we grow closer to Jesus, we face that tension. How can we feed our souls and touch others' lives for the kingdom? How can we discover a balance?

Men's Journal

Some anonymous friend
*   knowing my soul*
gave me a sub to a men's adventure magazine
*   no racy pics*
*   just kayaking killer rapids*
*   climbing mountains that kiss the stratosphere*
*   the latest and best gear*
*   to go anywhere*
*   to do anything*
*   money no object*

Perhaps the pics would have been more safe
For memories of youthful adventure flooded back
   solo cross-country motorcycle trips
      no destination but the ever-expanding horizon
   rappelling down a 190-foot bridge tower
      on a 110-foot rope
   climbing cliffs
      with no rope at all
   ready to go
      anywhere, anytime
Sparking regrets
   of too many years
   with too few adventures
      facing hostile church boards
      partners in ministry
      paying bills
      getting along
      getting by
Decades lost
   to the adventure
      that feeds my soul

In the most adventure-packed period of my life, I changed direction and opted for responsibility. For ministry. For touching the lives of others. For moving away from self-gratification to God gratification. And, yeah, you can tell I have some regrets. I miss a lot of the stuff I used to do. Yet I've reconnected with a good friend on Facebook from those days in Taos, and while those stories do get told, they've become rare. We share our current lives. God's role in us. Concerns about the state of the church and the country. Funny stories and memes. Inconsistencies both in others and ourselves.

So while some regrets continue, I wouldn't change that decision made decades back. Two truths have helped me. First, adventure and risk and an unknown future are normal in following Jesus. Four of those who became apostles had businesses, paid their bills, and supported their families. Then Jesus came into their lives. In Matthew 4:17, Jesus began to preach. In verse 18 he ran across Peter and Andrew. In verse 19 he challenged them: "Come, follow me…and I will send you out to fish for people."

They responded, "Well, we need to work out some details on wrapping up the business. We have contracts to honor." No, that's not the way it went down.

In verse 20: "*At once* they left their nets and followed him." You can read the next two verses, where Jesus challenged James and John in the same manner. They responded in the same way. Frankly, we don't know how much interaction they had with Jesus before this, but it doesn't seem like a lot. Risky behavior. An adventure. And it cost three of them their lives.

Jesus made this normative later, when a number of people expressed an interest in following him: "Still another said, 'I will follow you, Lord; but first let me go back and say goodbye to my family.' Jesus replied, 'No one who puts his hand to the plow and looks back is fit for service in the kingdom of God'" (Luke 9:61-62). That's hard core—get ready for a ride and don't look back.

The difference between my earlier adventures and these seemingly rash decisions? My adventures were to feed my own soul. These four did it to feed others'. Since then I may not have fully lived the wild, but it's not particularly been mild all the time either. Still doing solo back-country fishing trips. Motorcycle tours have hit 46 states and 3 countries. And church boards have sometimes risen to the level of adventure.

But I've been privileged to touch others, and I cherish that. You see, we only maximize our potential when we give our lives to serving.

To sacrifice: "Whoever wants to become great among you must be your servant, and whoever wants to be first must be your slave—just as the Son of Man did not come to be served, but to serve" (Matthew 20:26-28).

Following Jesus means we live the life he desires for us, the one that best allows us to serve his mission with who we are. So we come to the question: What can we do to best serve him? And once we've chosen, let's remember we made the best choice. The choice for adventure. For thrills. For uncertainty about much of our futures. The lesser choice isn't particularly a bad one. It's just not the best. For me, I had to leave behind some of the adventure. Others may need to abandon some of their need for security. Or comfort. Or financial success. Or...

KICK-STARTING THE APPLICATION

What value do you place on adventure and challenges? On the continuum of personal adventure or being responsible, where do you land? Try another continuum, personal preference at one end, serving God and others at the other. How have past experiences shaped those scores? Do you get a nudge from God you should move a bit on those lines?

What life does God most desire for you? How do you know that's his optimum for you? What changes would that bring? What benefits? What costs will it have? How will you handle regrets over the cost? (And they will come.) Will you be able to own the regrets and still own the greater good? How?

27

SMALL STEPS

When the Large Is Impossible, Do the Small

After a few days enjoying the delights and avoiding the decadence of New Orleans, I pulled into a rest area east of Beaumont, Texas, about midnight. A good time to quietly slip into some free lodging, but I discovered several facets of the South I hadn't fully experienced. First, the daytime heat and humidity didn't depart with the sun. The temperature felt like at least 90, and the humidity hovered just below becoming rain. Much too warm and sticky to crawl into a sleeping bag.

Second, bugs at night. A lot of them. In the darkness I couldn't see them, but they sounded and bit like mosquitoes. Much too painful to not crawl into the sleeping bag. Outside the bag, the bugs bit. Inside the bag, the sweat poured from my body. After three hours of switching back and forth and a futile striving to sleep, I gave up. I packed the bike at about 3 a.m. and headed west to meet some friends in El Paso: Somewhere over 800 miles, but 950 as my odometer later told me.

On virtually no sleep. I was just 26, and I thought I could drive hundreds of miles like that. Another lesson learned. After 20 minutes or so of riding and nearly dozing off, I stopped at the next rest area to walk and stretch—and discover a minor miracle. On this Labor

Day weekend, which I hadn't realized was a holiday, a CB radio group, REACT, offered coffee and donuts in exchange for a small, voluntary contribution.

The caffeine and sugar boost began to wear off after 30 minutes or so, just before another rest area that had been staked out by another REACT lifesaving group. That pattern repeated multiple times until dawn, when my body started the process of waking up. Rest areas became farther apart the farther I rode, but I could handle being awake now. So I survived riding after a night with no sleep, step by step, thanks to REACT.

But with the coffee and donuts I picked up a needed lesson on following Jesus. When the large journey looks impossible, success comes one small step after another. Riding 950 miles in one day on no sleep—impossible. Making it 20 miles to the next rest stop—possible. Being effective and productive as a follower of Jesus in your first year—impossible. Adding one trait at a time—possible. Let's explore that.

Begin at the End

My goal was to reach El Paso alive. The apostle Peter looks at some steps on our spiritual journey: "If you possess these qualities in *increasing measure*, they will keep you from being *ineffective* and *unproductive* in your knowledge of our Lord Jesus Christ" (2 Peter 1:8).

Focus on the concept of progress. We improve. That growth allows us to be effective in our faith, namely, that we don't become slow and lazy. We're involved. But we're more than active, we become productive. We make changes in the world. We see results from following Jesus. And we arrive safely in El Paso.

Just before this verse, Peter listed eight qualities that we should build on, step by step. Notice that we start with one, add the next, then another, and so on. Like climbing a staircase. Or taking advantage of REACT at each rest area: "Make every effort to *add to* your faith goodness; and to goodness, knowledge; and to knowledge, self-control; and to self-control, perseverance; and to perseverance, god-liness; and to godliness, mutual affection; and to mutual affection, love" (2 Peter 1:5-7).

Peter shows that progression. And we begin at the first rest area, because only then can we get to the next.

Faith

Belief begins our journey. Our commitment to Jesus as our Savior and Lord. I pulled out of that rest area with the belief I could reach El Paso. All the steps on our journey flow from our start, because "without faith it is impossible to please God" (Hebrews 11:6). But we continue to build on that.

Goodness

Once we get to know God, we're attracted to his character, to his virtue, to his goodness. That motivation begins to permeate our lives, and it brings a desire to shape our lives to match his goodness. How can we claim to say we love God if we don't want to become more like him?

Knowledge

So how do we grow in our goodness? We learn more about God from his Word and experience, and our foundation gains strength. Without this, we run the risk of taking side roads that lead nowhere. I saw quite a few of those in Central and West Texas that day, so we need a map and we need to study it. Passion for God by itself does little to move us along. In talking about the Jews, Paul said excitement won't get us there: "I can testify about them that they are zealous for God, but their zeal is not based on knowledge" (Romans 10:2).

Self-Control

Temperance, having a balance, allows us to say no to what moves us away from God and to say yes to what moves us closer.

Perseverance

When the going gets tough, genuine followers keep on keeping on. Even when discouraged, when the West Texas sun beats down and vultures circle overhead, we stay on track.

Godliness

These five qualities allow us to deepen our attachment to God, to increase how we value him. And his traits become more evident to others around us.

Mutual Affection

Here comes one of the best qualities. When we add all these qualities to our faith, our connections with people improve. We care more for them, we forgive them, and we build deeper transparency. And it all began with faith.

Love

Finally, we gain that *agape* love, the unconditional love for God and others. The love that most expresses the character of God. We give to others, not to benefit ourselves, but them. Our love covers a lot of sins in others (1 Peter 4:8).

Step by step, one rest area at a time, we reach an impossible goal.

Godliness

We share more and more of his character.

KICK-STARTING THE APPLICATION

Does growing into Christlikeness seem impossible? Which qualities do you do well in? Which do you most struggle in? What practical steps can you take to add more of these to your faith?

28

PUSH THE ENVELOPE

When a Challenge Trumps Ease

Until the trip in the last chapter, from Beaumont to El Paso, my longest ride in a day had been around 500 miles. So I figured two days on this El Paso run. But pulling out about 3 a.m. intrigued me, leaving well before my typical time to ride expanded the options for around 900 miles. So while enjoying coffee and a donut at a REACT rest area, I pulled out a map. Where could I stop for the night, about halfway before El Paso, that would provide something to explore?

San Antonio met the last target with the Alamo and Texas history and the River Walk. I'd like that, but it was only a third of the way, about 300 miles, with over 600 for the second day. West of San Antonio, nothing attracted me. A long ride. Hmm. A long day, how about doing the whole enchilada in one day? Not quite an Iron Butt, but a challenge. Almost doubling my previous personal best. So I called my friends in El Paso, committing myself to arriving that day.

Frankly, some memories have become vague. I hear East Texas has some beauty, but the darkness hid it. I mostly remember the rest areas. San Antonio had daylight, but then I just wanted to get through, so I only stopped for gas. With apologies to the residents, West Texas had more nothing than anyplace I've ever been. Not many cars (remember this was '74), but a lot of vultures circling overhead. I suspect they viewed me as lunch.

Vivid memories include having a sore butt, some high temperatures that made riding uncomfortable, a lot of coffee, and a tremendous sense of relief as I pulled into El Paso well after dark. Success!

So why did I push the envelope on this day? Why should we consider doing the same spiritually?

We Need Individual Challenges

I lean toward complacency. I could live in the Land of Least Resistance and just float downstream on its rivers. I know that and don't like it. I need challenges, like this ride, to blast me out of the comfort that restrains me. We only find our limits if we push them.

This trip demonstrated I could do much more than I'd thought—with a push. My life since has been an application of that lesson. But if we do what we've always done, what we know we can do, we'll never learn. We'll never grow. We'll never find the potential we can reach. Most great inventions come when a person pushes their limits. But these challenges far transcend the physical arena.

We Need Spiritual Challenges

I suspect many others share my tendency toward complacency in the spiritual arena as well, but a significant challenge can blast us into a greater arena of faith. For me, one arrived when God gently but insistently nudged me into the ministry. Up to that point, I worked and paid the bills, traveled a lot, but I had no professional purpose to drive me. No way to serve God grabbed me. But with the challenge of ministry, I left a place that almost matched heaven and went to seminary. Accepting that challenge from God changed the course of my life.

All my jobs since then have connected serving God and serving people. That decision forced me to yield my personal preferences and comforts. I grew up in faith.

God challenges each of us like that. He wants our best, and the method surprises me.

> His gifts were that some should be apostles, some prophets, some evangelists, some pastors and teachers, *to equip the saints* [all followers] *for the work of ministry,* for building up the body of Christ, until we all attain to the unity of the faith and of the knowledge of the Son of God, *to mature manhood, to the measure of the stature of the fulness of Christ* (Ephesians 4:11-13 RSV).

Later, I realized I erred a bit in accepting God's challenge, thinking only he wanted me in the professional ministry. He did, but he designed the Christian life to be ministry for all of us. With all the challenges and pains of ministry. He wanted me to build my life as a ministry, whether or not I was paid for it, whether or not I pastored a church. I should have emphasized ministry as a purpose long before.

What life-changing challenge does God give us all? To minister, to serve, to build the body of Christ. Because only then can we become mature, become Christlike. That challenge far exceeds riding a bike 950 miles in one day. Yet it brings rewards that transcend bragging about any number of miles. We become the person God desires.

The challenge of ministry forces a greater reliance on God. I've heard many speakers proclaim, "If you want to see God act, attempt something he wants that is bound to fail unless he's in it." When talking about handling difficult situations, Paul promised: "I know how to live on almost nothing or with everything. I have learned the secret of living in every situation, whether it is with a full stomach or empty, with plenty or little. For I can do everything through Christ, who gives me strength" (Philippians 4:12-13 NLT).

The more we accept difficult spiritual challenges, the more we see God's love and involvement. The more we see that, the closer we connect with him. The closer we connect, the more he can work in us.

So are you ready for a ministry challenge?

KICK-STARTING THE APPLICATION

What is the last personal challenge you addressed? What was the result? What did you learn about yourself? What was the last spiritual challenge you addressed? What was the result? What did you learn about yourself? About God? Do you sense God whispering a new challenge dealing with ministering? If so, how would that challenge help make a needed change in you?

29

A TOOL OR A JEWEL?

When Leaving a Bike Behind Is Good

I bought my slightly used '78 Gold Wing in '78 with just 6,000 miles on it. The original owner bought it as his only vehicle during one of SoCal's rare wet years, and he soon traded it for an Accord at the car dealer, so I got a great price on a great bike. Fast-forward 33 years and 70,000 miles: It barely limped into Deadwood, South Dakota, and then stumbled into a Sturgis bike dealer the next day.

No, the service manager replied, they didn't have time to diagnose it. They were jammed getting their own bikes prepped for the upcoming invasion for the annual rally there. He said it'd be two months before they could even look at it. I guess they had to take care of the local riders. All the other dealers said the same thing. So I was stuck in Sturgis, 1,300 miles from home, in the midst of a ride with three friends. Stuck with a bike that won't ride.

I could rent a pickup, slide the Wing into the bed, and pretend we rode Harleys. But I'd already decided to replace it. Two years before I'd had some trouble on a trip, and while I can turn a wrench, I'm more rider than wrencher. I wouldn't trust it on another long trip, and it wasn't fair to the other guys. So option one was gone.

I could sell the bike in Sturgis and head home on a bus or rent a car. But selling a nonworking bike didn't look optimal either. So I asked the guy about trading mine in for a used bike. A nice BMW sport tourer enchanted me—until I learned the price. Then I spotted a Kawasaki Vulcan 900 LT (light touring). It sported a good-sized windshield and leather saddlebags. They gave me a good price and added an allowance for the Wing for about what I'd have gotten back home (if it ran).

The salesman gave me a quick lesson or two on the features of the bike, I transferred my gear to the new scooter and took off to meet the guys. They'd left a few hours before, heading for the next hotel. So I had a solo ride on a new bike through the Black Hills, getting acquainted and adjusting. All of my earlier bikes had been Hondas, and none were V-twin cruisers like the Vulcan. The different style of handling and cornering surprised me some. It had straight-line stability like I'd never experienced, and it cornered like it wanted to stay in a straight line. The next two hours required a lot of attention for me to learn the bike and stay upright.

That night at dinner one of the guys asked if I missed the Wing, and my answer surprised me. Only then did I realize a truth about bikes and myself. Bikes are a tool, not a jewel. I loved having the Wing, and it brought a lot of great memories. But riding away, I didn't cry at its loss. Each bike is a tool for riding—and riding is the goal. So a good bike is one that lets me ride as I like. Every time I've changed bikes, the new one met that desire more effectively than the previous one.

All of this yields a cool story about life. We choose how to live our lives, then we find the tools to achieve what we want. But we don't allow the tools to become jewels. How does this apply to following Jesus? Let's look first at what Jesus said about the stuff of life, then we'll explore the implications:

Do not worry, saying, "What shall we *eat*?" or "What shall we *drink*?" or "What shall we *wear*?" [or what shall we ride]. For the pagans *run after* all these things, and your heavenly Father knows that you need them. But *seek first his kingdom and his righteousness*, and all these things will be given to you as well (Matthew 6:31-33).

Material Is Good

God created us as material beings with material needs and desires and pleasures. He knows we need them, like food and drink and clothing and housing—and bikes. Their essence is good when we enjoy them appropriately.

But they don't work well when we try to make them into the essence of life. Think of them as tools needed for life. Kind of like how I could leave one tool behind (the Gold Wing) for one that functioned better (the Vulcan). The prime importance doesn't come from being a tool but from what they help us accomplish.

Jesus encourages us to use these tools and not obsess so much over them that they interfere with following him. Too often we gain our identity, our self-worth, our status from our stuff. So let's use that and not run after them. Here's why.

God Is Better

Look at the last verse in another translation: "Seek the Kingdom of God above all else, and live righteously, and he will give you everything you need" (NLT). When we put God first, the stuff will come. But if we obsess over stuff, we may miss God entirely. Doesn't that sound a lot like society today? We've chased stuff and lost God. We've lost what only God can fully bring.

A sense of self-worth that flows from how he views us. A sense of purpose based on knowing an infinite and transcendent God. An identity that comes from knowing we're a child of God—not having a bike or a house or clothing that wears out.

Running after stuff won't give this. Only knowing God can.

KICK-STARTING THE APPLICATION

Do you give stuff too much importance in your life? Why? If other people examined your calendar and checkbook, would they see whether God or stuff is most important to you? Why is it easy to let stuff become too important? What can you do this week to focus less on stuff and more on God?

30

MORNING DEVOTIONS

How Majesty Enhances Humility

On a late June morning our group fired up the bikes and rode out of Kalispell, Montana, expecting great things at Glacier National Park, but some early indications didn't thrill us. The chill cut through our leathers and layers, and we had to endure 30 miles of mostly urban traffic before we approached the park. So far the shivers and the traffic frustrations revealed nothing awesome, just unpleasant. Then we entered the park.

The first ten miles or so were straight and slow and serene as we skirted Lake McDonald. Evergreens provided a covered archway. I relaxed. The frustrations of the earlier ride seeped away, and I sensed God's presence seeping into my soul.

Serenity decreased a bit as Lake McDonald gave way to McDonald Creek. In my beloved Sierras, creeks max at ten feet wide and often only reach about two feet. Trust me, McDonald Creek was a river. A rope bridge spanned the stream just below the falls, where the creek was a 30-foot-wide torrent rushing between rocks. The immense power reminded me of the power God used to create the world. I began to rest easy.

Things changed more at the Loop. The remnants of serenity turned into fear as we climbed a road gouged into the side of a sheer cliff. Narrow, with few side rails, the asphalt seemed about ten feet wide with a long fall if you slid off. So I tended to stay close to the center line. In the brief moments I could take to think, I remembered that God is so alien to us that he's worthy of fear. Not just respect, but fear, one greater than my fear of the road.

Slowly the fear gave way to awe. Not even the road could overpower the view of these massive mountains that looked as if they'd been carefully carved into the landscape. Moses must have walked these mountains, striking nearly every rock he saw. In one face of cut solid rock, maybe 150 feet long, two waterfalls tumbled, and water gushed from every square foot. For some reason, it was called the Weeping Wall. God utterly astounded me with his transcendence there.

On the return trip, half a dozen bighorn sheep played on a steep slope. One in particular picked her way down with more grace than Kobe Bryant (in his prime) soaring to the rim. Clearly, she was designed to do that, and she seemed to exult in it.

These morning devotions feed my soul. But why?

Nature Declares God's Glory

We humans can get full of ourselves in our cities, our own creation. Yet New York City's skyscrapers can't match the massive beauty of Glacier's mountains. I can understand how skyscrapers get built by people. Complex and difficult, yes, but they can't begin to compare to the aspens and firs and pines and cedars covering a mountain, where springs pour out water along with beauty. Nor the immensity of the forces that pushed the billions of tons of rocks toward the sky.

Some tasks totally exceed not just our ability but our imagination. And if they don't come from us, then from whom? "The heavens declare the glory of God; the skies proclaim the work of his hands.

Day after day they pour forth speech; night after night they reveal knowledge" (Psalm 19:1-2). The ability of a being to create this world boggles my mind.

When remodeling our Temecula house after we had rented it out for six years, I received a lot of compliments on the work. I'd worked in construction for a few years, knew a few things, did some research, and it turned out nice. But nothing like Glacier. The designer and contractor for that geological marvel far exceeded anything this human could do.

God's Glory Humbles Us

Yeah, a lot of us need regular humbling. And notice "us" is first-person plural. But because nature demonstrates a glory we can't begin to match, we realize we can't measure up to God. And in a good way that benefits us. We see a greater power that created the world, which puts us in our place.

"When I look at the night sky and see the work of your fingers— the moon and the stars you set in place—what are mere mortals that you should think about them, mere human beings that you should care for them?" (Psalm 8:3-4 NLT). One major reason I ride is to be humbled. God is so great and infinite and powerful and holy, and I am so small and finite and weak and sinful.

I wonder why he should care about me at all. But he does, and that is the miracle of grace. And when we see the transcendence of God in creation, when we experience that humility, then and only then do we understand what following is all about.

Humility Equals Worship

At its core, our worship acknowledges God's greatness, our need for him, and it gives us a principle that touches all we do and are. We yield to him. We center our lives on him. We obey him. We cherish him. We serve him. Why? Remember Keith Miller's line: "He's God and we're not."

Isaiah used the metaphor of a potter to describe this: "Yet you, LORD, are our Father. We are the clay, you are the potter; we are all the work of your hand" (64:8).

So as I ride, I worship. I see God's work. I realize he surpasses me. I acknowledge his love and grace.

KICK-STARTING THE APPLICATION

On a scale of 1 to 10, with 10 being the best, rank your humility. (No false humility, okay?) Do you intentionally put yourself in a position to best see God's glory? How often? How does that experience change your relationship with God? What are some things you can do to see the majesty of God?

31

DO THE RIGHT THING

Taking a Stand When It Might Cost Us

I hopped on the bike and rolled out of West Lafayette, Indiana, at about six in the morning, heading back to my beloved log cabin in Taos. I'd helped John get married, and yes, we pranked him. I convinced a bridesmaid who had a key to their apartment that I could be trusted. So we removed the labels from all the cans, put Kool-Aid in the shower heads, Saran Wrap under the toilet seats—all the typical stuff. But that's not the key part of the story.

The wide Kansas plains seemed flat, featureless, and boring. I confess I broke the law. My Honda 750 cruised easy at 90 to 100, chewing up the miles, and out of the hundreds of cars I flew by, I remember just two.

As I passed a modest sedan, the young woman driver looked frightened, as did the two young girls in the backseat. Just ahead was a '70s muscle car with four guys, all looking back at the woman. They slowed down so she could pass them, and then they sped up to pass her. When she pulled into a rest area, they waited at the next exit until she came along. I cruised along slowly, staying in sight, keeping an eye open.

Finally, she pulled over to the side, and the guys stopped about

100 feet ahead of her. I stopped too, about 100 yards ahead of them. They got out of their car. Heart pounding, I got off the bike. Images of being beaten half to death raced through my mind balanced with the scared look on her face. I was in good shape for a 28-year-old and had sparred with some Golden Gloves boxers, but I'm no UFC guy.

I soon learned the value of image. My Honda was slightly chopped with a custom paint job. Long hair flowed down to the shoulders of my leather riding shirt. The guys saw me, jumped back into their car, sped off in a 180 across the grassy median, and were gone in a proverbial cloud of Kansas dust.

Not wanting to scare her any more, I turned and walked back to my bike. She drove by with a grateful wave. I waited a moment to see if the guys might be coming back. They didn't.

Slowly my pulse returned to normal, and I pondered the risk I had taken. I'm not particularly courageous, but I knew I couldn't safely stay away. Four-to-one odds certainly didn't favor me, but I'd prefer bruises to a shamed conscience.

My point is this: Followers of Jesus should do the right thing. Regardless of the cost. Jesus gave us that principle, that we should count the cost, in a deeper application.

> Suppose one of you wants to build a tower. Won't you first sit down and estimate the cost to see if you have enough money to complete it? For if you lay the foundation and are not able to finish it, everyone who sees it will ridicule you, saying, "This person began to build and wasn't able to finish" (Luke 14:28-30).

So before we take on a task, we need to evaluate what it will cost and then decide. But look at how Jesus applied that principle: "In the same way, those of you who do not give up everything you have cannot be my disciples" (verse 33). He's talking about our faith.

So how does stopping on that Kansas roadside apply? I once read, "The only thing necessary for the triumph of evil is for good men to do nothing." Remember the story of the good Samaritan who risked his life to help an enemy? Explore that in Luke 10:25-37, and note that Jesus said a vital mark of loving God is to love people, and to love people means helping them to meet their needs as best we can. And sometimes doing good comes with a very real risk.

That makes me wonder, if we do nothing in the face of evil and wrong, are we truly good? Can we, as believers in a good God, play it safe when we're confronted with evil? Let's get more complicated. We can't fix all the wrongs in the world, so how do we decide when to act? How do we balance the potential risk against the possible gain?

KICK-STARTING THE APPLICATION

What areas might God be calling you to make a stand on that are biblically based? Could it be to protect others, to do the right thing, to stand for good when others seem to not care? What costs might come along if you did that? What keeps you from being willing to pay any costs? Should it? What standards do you use when determining to take a stand or not? And, most vital of all, how does God fit into all of this?

32

LAST LEGS

Setting Our Life's Pace

Mick and I left the rest of the riders in Sisters, Oregon, and headed home. Mount Shasta provided a motel room and a satisfying dinner at the Black Bear Diner, and then we traveled south on I-5 the next morning for an hour or so until Mick split off toward Susanville to return the bike he'd borrowed for the trip. (About a year earlier, thinking his riding days had ended, Mick gave his bike to his son-in-law. And then he realized he had a lot of miles yet to ride. So he borrows his old bike when he can.) I headed to Placerville, the jumping-off point to cruise Highway 49 through the old gold rush towns scattered along the Sierra foothills. It's a winding road with a lot of stops. I like finding things like Mark Twain's cabin, hitting a saloon, and exploring funky towns. It made it a long day before reaching a motel in Fresno.

That left about 240 miles to get home. Understand, I love riding. I mean, I *really* love riding. Sometimes a ride is a journey, like the earlier part of the trip. You take journeys slow enough to enjoy the countryside but fast enough to enjoy the bike. At other times it's all about a destination. Get there as soon as you can without killing yourself or getting ticketed. At Fresno the trip transitioned from a journey to a destination. Fresno to home in Thousand Oaks won't rate high on any list of scenic journeys. So eagerness to complete the trip took over.

I went down to breakfast at 6:15 for an early start, only to be delayed by a tour group with two buses of senior citizens already in line. An hour later I was on the freeway, where my speed kept creeping up, but *just* to keep up with traffic—honest!

On the old Ridge Route, Gorman offered a last gas stop, and I made a few calls over coffee and a doughnut. I arrived home by 11 a.m. after covering the 240 miles. Destination reached. Okay, I rushed it a bit. Math reveals all. But I finessed the last two legs of the journey to both see some fresh country and get home on time. And that finessing gives us a clue on following Jesus.

We need to look ahead and make some plans. I wanted to see the gold rush country, but I also wanted to get home the next day. So reaching Fresno required a long ride to make the last leg easier. Our spiritual lives are like that. Unless we look ahead to the last legs, we may not arrive satisfied.

Let's get personal, because I can see the last legs of my life. On this recent run I was 64, and I'll be 71 when this book releases. My life insurance agent recently told me to plan on 85 years. So what plans must I make to arrive with a smile? Financially? Ministry-wise? Health-wise? Character-wise? Intimacy with God-wise?

Some of you can see your last leg; some can't even imagine it yet. But thinking about how we want to finish allows us to craft a journey that will reach our destination. Avoid some plans and we minimize our chances of a successful arrival. Honestly, I wish I'd thought of this earlier, when just getting through consumed my thoughts and energy and resources. Up to my armpits in alligators, I thought little of draining the swamp. I could have invested in other options. I could have changed some behaviors and activities. Part of this last leg would have been easier to navigate.

God wants us to look at our last legs: "If only they were wise and would understand this and discern what their end will be!" (Deuteronomy 32:29). So target some issues critical to your arrival (like those mentioned above), and choose others that match you and your life.

Then begin to make some plans for your arrival at your last legs. Or how many miles do you want to travel before you check into a motel for the night, and do you have a reservation? What must you do now to get there by then? One more verse that has changed my life: "In their hearts humans plan their course, but the LORD establishes their steps" (Proverbs 16:9). Examine your life, your strengths and weaknesses, your desires. Like the first part of the verse, plan your route. But notice the last part—and hold onto the plans with a loose grip. Flex. Realize God may tweak your plans for your sake or for that of the kingdom. Most of all, live so God smiles when you arrive.

KICK-STARTING THE APPLICATION

Regardless of your age, have you done much thinking about the last legs of your journey? Why or why not? What role has God played in that? Do you have some targets for your arrival? Will your current activities help or hurt in achieving that? What changes can you make now that will benefit your last leg? Not just in regard to heaven, but where would you like your life to end up spiritually? Are you on the right track? How can you craft a better map?

33

GIVE A LITTLE

Compromising for Harmony

Some of my best experiences have come with wise compromise. A recent ride with Rich demonstrated that. We go back a long time, growing up at the same church in Long Beach, California, and we began riding together as soon as I got a bike 49 years ago. He rides a Harley, and I ride a Honda, but we're close. Honest. Yeah, we rag each other about our choices in good fun.

But our riding styles differ. A lot. I like to ride. A lot. I started this trip with a solo one-day ride of 630 miles, joyously pushing. A bit too goal-oriented, a major strength and weakness of mine. But on the day we connected in Taos, Rich got a late start and had logged 450 miles coming from his home in South Dakota. On a Harley. That is major iron-butt riding, and I told him I admired his endurance.

So rather than ride another 400 miles or so the next day on our projected route, we took the Enchanted Circle, a marvelous 80-mile loop from Taos to Eagle Nest to Red River to Questa and back to Taos. I've ridden the loop dozens of times. Less than two hours of riding time. Easy. It took us all day. We stopped just about every place we could and had something to eat or drink or view. He took a lot of pictures as a professional photographer. He intrigued me in the room at the Kachina Lodge that night as he transferred some pictures to his tablet and played with the effects. Me, I take a shot with my phone and I'm content.

At one stop, Rich leaned back on a bench, sighed, and smiled. "This is the kind of riding I love."

I smiled while thinking, *But let's get our butts on the seats!* Okay, I did enjoy the leisurely pace and gave up on riding more that day. I was okay with it. We rode and relaxed, rode some more and relaxed some more. I did appreciate the change of pace from the 5 a.m. departure of the day before leading to those 630 miles.

Rich's turn to compromise came on the next to last day. We left Springerville, Arizona, heading to Prescott and then to Blythe: 430 miles. But the weather experts predicted Blythe to reach 110 degrees, pure misery on two wheels. So we scheduled our riding hours to avoid the heat and spent several hours enjoying Prescott until dusk, so the desert would cool a bit before the last 160 miles to our motel.

Robert Burns shared some wisdom about best laid plans—they often get screwed up. We pulled into Blythe around midnight. The temperature exceeded 100, the room was about 90, and we had to hop in the pool to lower our body temperature.

I didn't say it, but that was the kind of riding I loved. Not the heat, but a decently long ride, trying to strategically handle conditions. And for one day Rich gave up the leisurely pace so we could evade the worst of the heat and make better time. The overall trip was excellent. We both got some of what we preferred and had great times and meals together and hit a lot of new roads.

What made the trip work so well? Both of us gave up something. Neither insisted on his way. To use biblical terms, we obeyed Paul's command to "submit to one another out of reverence for Christ" (Ephesians 5:21). Do you remember the basis for the first sin back in Genesis? Self-will. Be like God. Choose your path. Look out for number one. When we do this, other relationships suffer.

Submitting doesn't diminish the importance of our needs and desires. Rather, we care for others and their needs as much as ours. I cared enough for Rich, a longtime friend, to go slow and casual and relaxed for some of the ride. And Rich cared enough for me to pull a hard day when needed. If either of us had insisted on his way all the time, that would likely have been our last ride. But a long time ago we learned to flex and have had some good rides on a lot of roads.

Paul knew that when he encouraged us to aim for a balance: "Don't look out only for your own interests, but take an interest in others" (Philippians 2:4 NLT). We all have needs, and if we ignore them, we cannot meet those of others. If all we do is take care of ourselves, then we ignore others.

So we balance. We do some of both. That makes for good rides.

And isn't that the secret, not just for good bike rides, but for life? For our relationships? For our work? For our following Jesus? Submitting merely means we care about others and will yield our preferences to benefit the other. We also call that love. The normal Christian life.

KICK-STARTING THE APPLICATION

Think of a recent time when you gave up your desires to benefit another. What feeling did it give you? Did it impact the relationship? Now, let's flip a coin and think of a recent time when you knowingly did not yield your desires to benefit another? What result did that bring to you and to the relationship? Realizing we need to care for our own needs and those of others, how can you find a balance? When you yield or when you insist on your own way, what does that do to your relationship with God? What one specific act can you do this week to yield to the desires of another?

34

THE UPPER BEDROOM

Decreasing Selfishness Works

A day along the Oregon coast combined breathtaking scenery with bone-chilling cold. We'd headed west from Salem to Pacific City, on the coast, and then turned north to Tillamook, where we had lunch and sampled their famous cheeses. (Famous anyplace west of Wisconsin anyway.) The beauty of one stretch forced me to shout for joy, with ocean flats on our left while trees formed a canopy over our two-lane road. Clouds blocked the sun enough to give a gauzy sense of beauty and enough light to see it well.

In all the years of Gray Hog touring, this road neared the top of the list. But when we turned south, the sun took a nap and fog rolled in, and the world turned gloomy and damp and cold. At the time I was riding a Vulcan 900 LT with just a windshield and no fairing. I froze. I've crossed the Sierra during a winter snowstorm on a bike with neither fairing nor windshield, but this chilled me more. The moisture cut to the bone. My buddies had mostly Gold Wings with full fairings and windshields, and even they were cold.

When we came to Lincoln City we needed coffee for some instant internal warmth along with lunch, and the Indian casino there yielded both. During lunch, the sun woke up for about five miles and then went back to snoozing. We went back to freezing.

We had a target: a vacation rental in Newport. Jerry had some church friends who offered it to us as long as we laundered the sheets and towels we used. So being kind and appreciative bikers, we brought sleeping bags and towels to save riding time.

As we pulled up to the property, Jerry called dibs on the upstairs bedroom. That was only fair, since he got us the place for free. After 15 minutes of figuring how to safely turn off the alarm, he ran upstairs to claim the master suite. Next, Mick and I walked in downstairs and threw our bags on the twin beds in the first bedroom. We wanted a decent room and grabbed the first we saw to not get left out. Gary came in last and found the master suite, a large room with a king bed and its own bath.

After unpacking our bags, we went upstairs to see Jerry's prize. No upstairs master suite. In fact, no bedroom at all. Just a nice kitchen, a marvelous great room with a phenomenal view (after the fog cleared), and a love seat with a pullout bed.

Yes, we ragged him about it. He admitted, "I got screwed." As an English teacher and an author and a long-term friend who loved sarcasm, I let him know his grammar was wrong. "I got screwed" is passive voice, indicating something done to him. "Jerry, you should have used the active voice." He grinned. "Okay, I screwed myself."

God tends to turn things upside down. Jerry, so eager to get the best room, wound up with the worst. Gary, letting all the others choose first, had the best room. Jesus proclaimed a paradoxical value for his kingdom: The first will be last and the last be first. But all four of us follow Jesus, and three of us maneuvered for first. We failed the test, didn't we?

Jesus' call for radical discipleship goes against our grain. We look out for number one, we let ambition drive our lives, and we think we're doing okay. We're not. You see, the story didn't just indict Jerry, a pastor and sincere believer. Mick, an elder, and I, also a pastor, got it too. A verse I used a few weeks ago comes back to haunt me: "Everything that does not come from faith is sin" (Romans 14:23).

Maybe all of us should think before we act. *What would Jesus have me do? How can I best serve? Am I willing to pay a price for serving?*

All followers of Jesus need to run each decision through the grid: *Am I serving myself or others? Am I trying to get ahead or yield?* Perhaps the most frightening version of that question might be, *Am I serious in trying to live like Jesus?* I suspect—no, I'm convinced, Jesus would have let us all scurry for the best rooms and taken whatever was left. Gary met that test and got the best. Ironic, huh?

KICK-STARTING THE APPLICATION

In what areas do you find it most difficult to go last? What in your soul causes that vulnerability? Can you come up with a strategy for yourself that will remind you to consider how to prioritize serving when you're faced with selfishness? How can you find a balance between meeting your own valid needs and considering the needs of others? Read and ponder Philippians 2:4 (NLT): "Don't look out only for your own interests, but take an interest in others, too."

35

500 MILES OF MISERY

Don't Quit Too Soon

Honestly, I never thought about stopping or turning back. But 500 miles of misery to start a motorcycle trip did wear on me. The garage door dropped down just after 5 a.m., and I'd slogged through 80 miles of metropolitan Los Angeles congestion before meeting Mick and Brad at the Cajon Pass on I-15. The metro freeways do not qualify as favored riding for me, but the metro yielded to the desert, and the desert brought heat, and by the time we got to Vegas, the temperature bumped 100. At 11 a.m.

Lunch at In-N-Out cooled us a bit, but the temperature outside had moved up to 105, and we had 170 miles between us and the air-conditioned room we'd reserved for that night. The temperature continued to climb with the altitude until it maxed at 109. About 30 miles from Cedar City it began to cool, and 99 degrees felt almost chilly. Note the "almost." Our motel's cool pool finished lowering our body temperature, and we walked to a nice café next door for dinner. Better than getting back on the bikes.

That night we needed to determine the next day's route to meet Jerry and Todd in Richfield, Utah, about 100 miles to the north. Yearning to escape the interstate, Highway 14 intrigued us: 41 miles

142

of mountain roads before hitting Highway 89 to the east. We gambled the temperature wouldn't be bad, but we missed seeing the pass elevation: 9,896 feet. When we started the next morning, it wasn't too long before we stopped to put on more gear to handle the cold, which soon dropped to 36 degrees—73 degrees less than just the day before. Mick's face almost froze, and my fingers were numb. We didn't have enough gear to deal with the cold.

But Highway 14 was totally worth it. Still drained from the day before and almost frozen, we were nonetheless captivated by the rocky, multicolored cliffs, the lush forests and meadows, the beautiful pale green aspen, and the vistas we glimpsed as we crested hill after hill overlooking wide, green valleys below.

So what's the hook for spiritual formation? Those two days provided a metaphor for spiritual living. Some pain, some gain. Some blah, some beauty. Don't expect that either will be all you experience. Don't get too discouraged by the misery—it won't last. Don't get too excited by the beauty—it won't last either. Granted, the ratios will vary, depending on the circumstances of our lives and what we most look for. But we all get each.

Expect the difficult. It always accompanies life. We don't generally view the two certainties of life—death and taxes—with smiles. Back in the Jesus movement days I appreciated *The Jesus Person Pocket Promise Book*, a collection of promises our Lord gave. I don't remember this one being there: "I have told you these things, so that in me you may have peace. *In this world you will have trouble*. But take heart! I have overcome the world" (John 16:33). All the apostles but one died as martyrs for their faith. None made any money; all faced hard times and opposition.

Life overall comes with the promise of difficulty, as God promised Adam and Eve and their descendants: "Cursed is the ground because of you; through painful toil you will eat food from it all the days of your life. It will produce thorns and thistles for you, and you will eat the plants of the field. By the sweat of your brow you will eat your food until you return to the ground" (Genesis 3:17-19). A fallen world brings pain and trouble and difficulty. Our world.

Also, expect the pleasure. The world God created and gave us is good. It produces our food; it brings beauty into our lives. Enjoy the sweet juice of a plum that runs down your chin with your first bite. Enjoy the delicate art of leaning into a turn on your bike as you balance speed, gravity, and centripetal force. Let your spirit soar when you see a clear sky of blue. Embrace the humility that comes when you ride next to the mountain mass that dwarfs you. God placed good in this world for us to enjoy and take advantage of. And the more we focus on the delightful parts of life, the more our spirits soar.

So how do we respond? When the path gets boring or painful, don't quit. Endure it for the goal. Realize hard times make us strong *and* reveal the strength we have. If metro LA and the desert heat had caused me to turn back, I would have missed the glory of Highway 14. I discovered more endurance than I thought I had.

That translates to following Jesus as well. When in difficulties, as we lean on him, we can handle far more than we anticipated.

Also realize that all aspects add up to life. Just as surely as God created that gorgeous country around Highway 14, he also created the stark landscape around I-15. Both shout—or at least whisper—that a magnificent creator designed it all. Let's try to enjoy as much of his grace as we can, okay?

KICK-STARTING THE APPLICATION

Have you experienced that blend of agony and ecstasy from life? Does one ratio seem to dominate in your life? How do you typically respond to both states? Do you sometimes go to the extremes of excitement or misery? For you, what best keeps you keeping on through the hard times? How can you use both to deepen your closeness to Jesus?

36

KISSING CONCRETE

When Good Seems Invisible

Snick. With the push of a button, the garage door descended. *Snick.* With another button, my newest acquisition—a 2005 Honda ST1300—purred into life. This would be my first long-break-in-get-used-to-it ride before heading to Glacier National Park the next month. By day's end, Brad, Sean, and I had ridden 340 miles through the mountains and valleys and beaches, the ranches and farms and cities of Ventura and Kern Counties. I renewed a friendship from decades earlier and reconnected with Brad from our summer touring group. But now all of us lay face down, kissing concrete, with multiple pistols pointed at our heads and tense faces behind the triggers.

We may have been speeding (emphasis on the word "may"), but it wasn't enough to warrant six police cars and what seemed like 250 officers on the scene (or at least 10), all of whom had pistols in their hands. Honestly, I didn't feel guilty about anything. We'd been moving with a lot of traffic on the Pacific Coast Highway. But now a lot of fear invaded my heart. I remembered the 1991 beating of Rodney King by police officers in Los Angeles and Malcolm Gladwell's account of the 1999 police shooting of Amadou Diallo in the Bronx. When Diallo was asked to identify himself, he reached for his wallet, and 41 bullets erupted. One mistake today, one unintentional move, and we all might die there in the concrete. I honestly had no clue about why.

All three of us ended up with our own personal cop. Each asked if we had any weapons. I confessed to having a Swiss army knife. The cop asked me to carefully take it out of my pocket and remove the chain holding it to my belt loop. He took it, and then another cop yelled, "Gun!" Their tension magnified. Sean, a law enforcement officer, had a holstered pistol that his cop saw before he could tell him. Our tension magnified.

What caused it? Some guy in a pickup with road rage issues filed a false report that three bikers flashed a gun at him on the freeway. I had been riding alongside Sean when this supposedly happened, and I knew he hadn't taken the gun from its holster. Apparently, the wind blew his T-shirt up enough to reveal the holstered pistol. (He had a valid carry permit.)

Obviously, the situation worked out. They finally cleared us, and during the incident I had an opportunity to talk about God to my cop, a good guy who seemed to want more from his faith. Get this, I'm handcuffed with my hands behind my back, sitting sideways in the back seat of his cruiser, talking about God and healthy churches! All while I was also in great discomfort and significant fear this entire time.

So what's the point of telling this story? I talked to someone about Jesus, and that was good. We lost three hours of our lives and almost peed our pants—not so good. I'm still a bit unclear about the deeper reasons why all this happened, but I have several suggestions about what we can learn from it.

Maybe the key is understanding that life can change on a dime. Some say we never know how we'll react in a particular situation until it arrives. I'm not so sure. I've had a number of close calls over the years that have forced me to think about events that could have ended fatally. I'm 71 now, much closer to my end than my beginning. I have no desire to die, but all those thoughts helped me not freak out when this happened. The cops had a report of three bikers flashing a gun on the freeway. A serious felony. Their lives were at risk, and I understood why they would be tense. But the result could have been much different.

We plan, and that's good. But let's not get too adamant about our future plans.

> Look here, you who say, "Today or tomorrow we are going to a certain town and will stay there a year. We will do business there and make a profit." How do you know what your life will be like tomorrow? Your life is like the morning fog—it's here a little while, then it's gone. What you ought to say is, "If the Lord wants us to, we will live and do this or that." Otherwise you are boasting about your own pretentious plans, and all such boasting is evil (James 4:13-16 NLT).

All my future plans could have ended on that road. Although we have no assurances of how our lives will go, we do possess God's presence. He's with us in the changes. I sensed that throughout this encounter.

Second, this reinforced the importance of honesty. That guy in the pickup lied by making a false report, and it could have resulted in a loss of lives. Mine. My friends'. For followers of Jesus, we have a high command: "Instead, we will speak the truth in love" (Ephesians 4:15 NLT). Funny how Paul linked truth telling and love, isn't it?

Third—and clearly—let's grab every chance we have to tell people about Jesus. To steal a line from the movie *Top Gun*: "I had the shot...so I took it." The cop didn't understand who the real captive was. I had a captive audience to graciously share Jesus with. Handcuffed, sitting sideways in the back seat of a cop car, I lived out the scripture: "If someone asks about your hope as a believer, always be ready to explain it" (1 Peter 3:15 NLT). When the officer learned I had been a pastor, he opened the topic, and we had a good conversation.

Best of all, through it all, I had peace. In part, even if it all went south, I knew where I'd be seconds after the first shot. More so, I deeply felt the presence of God.

KICK-STARTING THE APPLICATION

This question has to be obvious: Have you thought about how quickly life can change? Have you pondered how you might react if certain situations arose? More specifically, how would you react if death were a valid result? I encourage you to think about how you would respond. I suspect that increases the odds of that response being a good one.

37

ROAD MAPS

GPS or Paper, Have a Reliable Map

Typically, our biker crew meets on the first day of our ride, but a scheduling conflict required me to leave a day later than the rest of the guys on a trip to the Black Hills of South Dakota. This led to two days of solo riding for me before I rendezvoused with the rest of the Gray Hogs in Rexburg, Idaho. The weather dealt a heavy hand of heat of more than 100 degrees in Las Vegas, and then threw a joker down on me. After the temperature dropped a lot in St. George, a storm blew in. The wind, coming at me from the front and the side, forced me into a heavy lean to stay upright. And the heavy rain forced its way past my fairing and into my eyes, making the road nearly invisible.

Cold and wet and whipped, I stopped much earlier than planned at the first clean motel I found with enough overhang to keep my bike out of the rain. I think the town was Santaquin, because much of that day is a blur in memory. An indoor spa and a hot shower returned a semblance of warmth to my body, and the next day, under a clear sky, I jumped on I-15 and headed north, intending to cut off at Highway 25 north to Rexburg. I was still tired from fighting the weather of the previous day and in a hurry to make up some lost time. When I came across some road construction, I missed the turnoff. But I made good time on I-15, thinking it was Highway 25. Quite good time.

Although the towns I passed didn't seem familiar, I kept going. I was going too quickly, and I didn't want to waste any time by stopping to check my map. Finally, I was concerned enough to pull over, and I discovered the mistake I'd made 30 miles before. Fortunately, a road led straight east to Rexburg, but it was 30 wasted miles away. Now, let's talk about another story that leads to the lesson.

Not long ago a Facebook friend sparked a challenging discussion when she posted an article titled "Sick of Christianity?" The male author seemed to want to rewrite the Bible and condemn judgmentalism in the church in order to justify his gay lifestyle. Let's not get sidetracked on that issue. What I want to share about that is a comment by my friend Roland Peachie that showed keen insight: "He's just a sinner without remorse...who wants acceptance [and] is not looking for a way into heaven."

What's the connection between my story of missing the turn and Roland's comment? We each need to first decide what destination do we desire? Really, it breaks down to two options. Do we value loving and knowing God the most or do we value doing whatever we desire? The two cannot coexist. Choosing God means saying no to ourselves. A lot. Saying yes to ourselves means we can do whatever we desire and can afford or get away with. We do what we want, but we really don't want Jesus. He himself made that distinction: "If you love me, you will keep my commands" (John 14:15). The clear implication is that not wanting to obey reveals a lack of love for him.

Then we choose the right map. My AAA map of the Western United States gave me the right directions to reach my destination. If we choose God, we also have the map we need: "All scripture is inspired by God and profitable for teaching, for reproof, for correction, and for training in righteousness, that the man of God may be complete, equipped for every good work" (2 Timothy 3:16-17 RSV). Frankly, the Bible doesn't answer all my questions. According to NASA, dark matter and energy make up 95 percent of the universe, as determined by the movement of stars.[1] Now, does that correspond to God's spiritual world? The Bible doesn't say, but it still gives a good road map to knowing God!

Now, if we choose to primarily follow our desires, almost any road map will do. But let's not redraw God's road map and assume it will still lead us to him. You know what assuming does, so be careful here. That's the point Roland made.

Next, once we've chosen our destination and grabbed the right map, then we need to follow it. My mistake was that I checked out the map before hopping on the bike and assumed I would remember it. But missing that turnoff took me off my route. Sound like our spiritual lives sometimes? Frankly, we'll all go off the rails at times. Even though obedience is essential for following Jesus, let's not get into thinking we must be perfect. He is; we're not. The apostle John made that clear: "If we claim we have no sin, we are only fooling ourselves and not living in the truth" (1 John 1:8 NLT).

So when we miss the mark, or sin, we fix it. The next verse in 1 John 1 adds to our road map: "If we confess our sins to him, he is faithful and just to forgive us our sins and to cleanse us from all wickedness" (NLT). When we go off track, we need to admit it. We also need to check the map and get back to our route. I wasted 30 miles but I fixed it. Again, like our spiritual lives.

The good news here is that when we choose God, he gives us a road map we can rely on. And we can get back on track.

KICK-STARTING THE APPLICATION

Think back on a recent time you got off track. Why did it happen? What is your desired destination spiritually? What's your road map to get there? What caused you to choose the one you did? Was it the concept of absolute truth or subjective truth? What role does the Bible play here? If you chose God's Word as your road map, how often do you check your route with the map? How can you better learn to read the map? How do you best sense you're off track?

38

ROOTS

When Looking Back Helps

My annual cross-country biker group calls itself the Gray Hogs in an allusion to Tim Allen's movie *Wild Hogs*. There are two prime requirements to be a Hog, and neither one is that you need to belong to the Harley-Davidson Owners' Group. Just pack on a few extra pounds and sport some gray hair. Oh, yeah, and ride a bike and get along with the charter members.

Old totally dominated a day on a recent ride to the Taos, New Mexico, area. We visited the country's oldest continuously occupied residence, Taos Pueblo, which dates back to AD 1000. A bit later in Santa Fe we explored the country's oldest church, the 1610 San Miguel Mission (I snuck up and rang the bell before learning they allowed it), the oldest seat of government from colonial days (the 1610 Palace of the Governors), and what some claim to be the country's oldest residence, the 1646 De Vargas Street House.

In comparison, I felt younger with every stop along the way. Ironically, all remained in good, functional condition probably better than I. We then rode up Pecos Canyon to our cabin. We passed a decaying cabin dating back to the 1800s. Its condition didn't match the older structures—falling down and obviously unoccupied.

But all this caused me to ponder the past. Particularly our roots. I appreciate the efforts of those who came before. They often built well. They searched out a new country and found freedom and fresh ways of living. That led me to conclude the following: To comprehend our present and prepare for our future, we need to understand our past. That allows us to effectively strategize for our best future. That applies to countries, churches, and individuals. We can only fully engage others when we appreciate our past and their past. That enhances understanding.

Obviously, historical roots don't chain us to what previous generations accomplished. Change happens for good and bad. But the past lays the bricks of the present building, and before we change the structure, we need to know the foundation.

First, our country built a foundation with bricks of faith from the Judeo-Christian tradition. My bachelor's degree is in history, my teaching arena was American literature, and we can't evade that Judeo-Christian foundation. But we're changing. Some say we're now a post-Christian nation. Certainly, that's the current direction. Those positive about those changes need to grasp the past just as those who are negative need to grasp the present. Only then can we wisely interact with one another.

So how do we follow Jesus in a secular culture? Let's avoid trying to resurrect the past, but let's understand the present in order to influence the future. I've found there are many benefits in discussing the source of values. Graciously ask people where they get their values. Do they accept any form of absolute values? Why? Get them thinking about the chaos that results when everyone chooses their own right and wrong.

Second, many people are depressed over the shrinking size and influence of today's church. History reveals this is not a new issue. Just read the book of Judges. God's people received spiritual direction from a judge. When he died, society departed from God and experienced the awful consequences of their moral relativism. And came back to God: "In those days Israel had no king; all the people did whatever seemed right in their own eyes" (Judges 17:6 NLT).

Not a single congregation mentioned in the New Testament still exists today, but the body of Jesus—the church—still does. And will. "I say to you that you are Peter (which means 'rock'), and upon this rock I will build my church, and all the powers of hell will not conquer it" (Matthew 16:18 NLT). So relax, God remains in charge of his church. And hell cannot conquer it. Doesn't knowing that keep us from being overly discouraged?

Third, we individuals need to know how events and people from our past have shaped us. Here's a silly example. My step-grandfather designed railroad bridges, and his work frequently took him away from home. Because his wife, my dad's mom, didn't much like to cook, she took the family out to eat most of the time. Eating out was a financial extravagance she gladly paid. But dad grew up hating to eat out, and we rarely did. He cherished his stable home. As an adult, I love going to coffee shops and reading and writing poetry and observing people. My grandmother shaped my dad, who shaped me. And often we moved to the other end of the spectrum in response.

But what earlier spiritual experiences influence us today? Earlier teachings? Harmful experiences with others in church? If we're aware of them, we can begin the process of moving beyond them and healing. Or we can build on them to grow more.

The roots of a plant will either limit or help the plant's growth. As we examine our roots, we expand our ability to grow closer to God.

KICK-STARTING THE APPLICATION

Spend some time pondering how your past has influenced you. What were some of the major positive events and people? Specifically, how did they shape you? Do the same with any negative issues. Do you know much about how your parents and grandparents shaped your character and faith? If you can, get them to tell you about their lives, and I suspect you'll find some nice surprises. Do you see any family themes that transcend gencrations? And most important of all, how does all of this shape your attitude toward God and your faith in Jesus?

After you've done this and based on what you've found, spend some time meditating and praying about how to deepen your walk with God. What can you share with the rest of us who are on that journey?

39

TAKING CHANCES

When Risks Don't Reward Us

Neither AAA maps nor locals always give us good information. The Gray Hogs pulled out of Cortez, Colorado, early one June morning with Telluride in our sights. The ride got a bit chilly, so we pulled off to the side of the sparsely trafficked road to pull off our jeans and put on long johns and insulated pants. The brief exposure to the cold paid off, but the temperature didn't get any better as we cruised into the town surrounded by the San Juan Mountains at 8,700 feet. About 30 elk calmly grazed at the outskirts.

Needing an infusion of internal warmth, we found Suzie's Coffee House, only to meet Sal, the husband of the owner and a fellow biker. After some talk about our bikes, he asked if we'd heard of Gateway, the hidden secret of Colorado and the best bike ride in the state. Now, Colorado's beauty is second to none, so that got our attention. Our original route was to take Highway 145 northwest to Placerville, Highway 62 northeast to Ridgway, then US 550 north to Montrose, and then head east to Gunnison, with a side trip to Crested Butte. He suggested changing our route to 145 to 141 to 550. (You'll have to know the area or break out a map here.)

He claimed the road was designed for bikes, and the best part was a canyon with thousand-foot walls of almost vertical sandstone, with just the road and a stream at the bottom. We checked the map, which marked it as scenic. The Hogs tend to trust local bikers, so off we went. The results?

In the terms of gambling terminology, we went bust. We traveled an extra 130 miles and had to skip Crested Butte. Just about *all* Colorado roads are good for bikes, but only 10 miles of this one made our eyes bug out. For lunch we stopped at the Gateway Resort, where I paid $8 for an apple and a small pastry. The glass of water was free, though. Right after lunch we ran into rain and hail, where one stone deftly evaded my windshield and nailed my chapped lower lip.

Now, would we do it again? That depends. Knowing what I know now, having ridden the road—absolutely not. We missed more gorgeous country than we saw, rode three hours longer than we planned, were ripped off at lunch, and hit a strong storm we would have missed. But—if we were in the same situation again, not knowing the road but hearing good stuff from a local rider and seeing it on the AAA map—we'd all do it in a clichéd heartbeat.

So how does this connect to following Jesus? Think of this story as a metaphor about taking risks and failing.

Some of the best change points of my life spiritually came when I took a big risk without a glimmer of the outcome. At the age of 27, with a good job and great prospects for advancement, I resigned and drove off in my van for Colorado to build a new life. I had some savings, but not a lot. I would need to find a job quickly, yet I made a short detour to Taos. Within three days God arranged not only a job but housing as a resident caretaker for an unused guest ranch in the mountains.

That all came from visiting the First Baptist Church of Taos, which then challenged me to get back into ministry. But playing it safe would have kept me in Long Beach. That risk paid off, and the arc of my life changed forever.

Frankly, many risky choices cost us. We crash and burn. That happened with some ministry choices. At one church, I placed a member in a key ministry role that well suited his gifts, only to discover the gifts didn't match his character. His maneuvering contributed to my leaving that ministry. A risk that backfired.

Another time I felt God's call to plant a new church. One with no outside financial support or people—not the wisest way to do it! But despite the risk, we assembled some key people on the team, started it, reached a lot of people who didn't know Jesus, and that became the most fruitful and encouraging church I ever served.

Taking risks wisely, under the guidance of God as we can best figure it out and obtaining good counsel, can provide a nice payoff, one that would never have existed without the risk. But I've also learned that even when we do it right, when we do our due diligence, we can fail.

Yet even when the risk turns out to be a loser, God's presence and love and comfort remains. Or they will grow to match the need. And we learn.

Before cell phones provided GPS guidance, I purchased a Garmin GPS to get verbal directions to new locations. It became an annoyance by constantly saying "Recalculating" whenever I didn't follow its instructions, but it provided reassurance when taking risks. We can recalculate and get back on track. And God plays a key role too: "The mind of man plans his way, but the LORD directs his steps" (Proverbs 16:9 NASB).

When we crash and burn, we lean on God and recalculate. We don't give up riding because the risk didn't work out. We don't give up following because it didn't work out as we hoped.

KICK-STARTING THE APPLICATION

Do you lean toward the risk-taking or security side of faith? Why? Think carefully on this one. Is it influenced by your family heritage, experiences, or what others have taught you? What risks have paid off for you? Which risks didn't work out? What have you learned from each? What role does God play in the level of risk you're willing to assume? Should you increase the number of risks you take?

40

WILDLIFE DETECTED

Seeking Signs

Naw, this chapter won't direct you to any wild parties in your neighborhood! Let's talk about another kind of wildlife: deer. In 43 years of riding bikes, much of it in the mountains, I never gave a thought to deer darting across the road and trying to knock me off the bike. Then, a couple of years ago, in Libby, Montana, the Gray Hogs talked to a local who had hit 23 deer. Killed 17 of them. That gave me pause. Less than a week later on that same ride, on the road to Eureka, a deer bolted in front of Brad, who had no chance to avoid the collision. After the life flight to appropriately named Mercy Medical Center in Redding, doctors tended to multiple broken ribs, a collapsed lung, a broken collar bone and shoulder blade, and a number of abrasions. A plate with nine screws now resides in his shoulder. He still rides, but that incident got my attention.

So I was particularly cautious a few years later on a solo trip when I left Pagosa Springs at 5:30 a.m. with hot coffee in the cup holder. Some heat was needed with the temperature dropping to 35. Deer tend to travel at that time of day, so I kept looking at the sides of the road, remembering Brad. Then a sign read "Wildlife Detection Zone Ahead." I had no clue what that meant. I'd seen "Deer Crossing" signs in abundance, but I had no idea what a detection zone was.

A few miles later a sign flashed "Wildlife Detected." I slowed—and saw nothing. Within a few minutes another sign came on, and again I slowed, looking for a deer. Nothing. Suddenly a big doe ran just in front of me from my left, heading right. I missed her by no more than ten feet, although that was likely five feet. If I hadn't slowed down for that sign, I'd have played hit-and-slide. For the next 50 miles I crawled through the mountains, desperately searching each blade of roadside grass for deer. I now fully understood what a Wildlife Detection Zone is all about.

So the spiritual hook? Clearly, how great it would be if we had "Temptation Detection" signs with flashing lights to get our attention before we headed into a danger zone. Think of something like Google Glasses that project a heads-up display: "Temptation Detected." Wouldn't that make following Jesus much easier? Especially if it specified the temptation and sin!

Yeah, this is simplistic, but we have that warning system. Mark Twain is credited with a good line about it: "It's not the things in the Bible I don't understand that bother me. What bothers me is what I understand and don't do." But that comes with a kicker— Twain lived at a time when most knew what the Bible taught, and those values made up the value system of the culture. Obviously, not everyone followed the rules, but they at least knew them.

And while people today all acknowledge that right and wrong exist, they define each as they desire. We've moved away from absolute values into a world of relative ethics, where each individual chooses. Even followers of Jesus often either don't know or ignore biblical values. My friend Bill has attended a solid local church for nearly a decade, yet he lives with his girlfriend. Does he not know or care?

For a "Temptation Detected" warning to work, we need to know the road map of temptation and sin—the one that God our Creator provided. But just knowing won't protect us unless we slow down when we see the flashing signs. If I had decided to blow through that morning and ignore all the signs, both for speed and wildlife, then nothing about the signs would have helped me one bit. If I'd hit 80 mph even after I saw the 55 limit, I'm at risk. Deservedly.

So to best follow Jesus, we pay attention to the signs with a willingness to change our speed. Slowing down at that sign near Durango saved me from a lot of pain. And expense. And embarrassment. Underlying all of our discussion about signs, we need to grasp that God our Creator knows best. That means we prioritize following his Word, even when it may not make short-term sense or match our desires.

Let me suggest we create our own "Temptation Detected" signs, unique to us. Here's what I mean. Based on our experiences or how most of us learn (unfortunately), we have a pretty good idea of our triggers, our weak areas. These may not even be sin, but with that step we typically take the next that goes beyond temptation into sin. So rather than continuing to blast ahead at full speed, we must slow down. We pray. We ponder. We change our route a bit. Why? Very simply, hitting sin at full speed can bring more damage than Brad experienced.

KICK-STARTING THE APPLICATION

Think first about the concept of sin detection zones. How well do you know God's directions in the Bible? I see it as God's operations manual for life—and he knows better than we what works and what doesn't. It's not so much a rule book as it is a guide book, but we usually don't have time to stop and find an appropriate verse. So what can you specifically do to better understand his guidelines? What level of commitment will you make to follow God's values when they contradict what you'd prefer to do?

Last, can you craft some temptation-detected zones specific to you? Are you aware of your vulnerabilities and what increases their level? Are you willing to become more rigorous in staying farther from sin by changing your behaviors earlier? Feel free to talk about this with some trusted fellow riders. Be accountable—that helps.

41

PUKE AND RALLY

Never Give Up

The Gray Hogs pulled out of our lodging in Santa Rosa, California, around 7 a.m. in mid-May, intending to head north on Coast Highway 1. We were about 30 miles from Jenner, right on the coast, and the damp cold caused us to stop there for coffee. After we defrosted, we hopped on the coast route, but the cold never let up. Another 30 miles and we had to stop again, this time at an old general store and gas station at Stewart's Point. Ironically, we felt colder inside the dark building than in the sunshine outside, so we migrated there.

Just as one of the guys noticed a flyer for a Navy Blue Angels air show 70 miles up the road in Fort Bragg, we heard a roar overhead, looked up, and glimpsed a very fast blue jet flying south, just above the highway. Our hearts hummed in tune with the Blue Angel until it disappeared. About a minute later it reappeared, heading east from the ocean, right over our heads. And not far over. As he approached the coastal mountains, he shot straight up for a good distance, then pulled a 180 and headed back straight down. At what seemed to us like 100 feet above the ground, he did an almost 90-degree turn and disappeared. For good this time.

We thrilled over our personal Blue Angel show. It hooked me, and

I yearned to ride a military jet. A few years later I officiated at a wedding for a Top Gun instructor and all but begged for a ride. Recently I talked to a family member who did public relations for the Thunderbirds, the Air Force demonstration squadron. She coordinated rides for celebrities (somehow I didn't qualify) and said the odds were 50-50 for the celeb to puke during the ride. Yes, she's ridden, and yes, she puked.

So the team prepares the passenger on how to avoid it, and then they share their slogan: Puke and Rally. If you feel like it's gonna happen, grab the bag, and then get back on track. Honestly, I'd give my left arm to ride in one of these jets, and if I puked, I'd certainly want to rally to be able to enjoy the rest of the flight.

What a helpful metaphor for life. Setbacks and problems and trials will hit us. If a biker hasn't gone down, eventually he will. Our local paper recounts at least one motorcycle riding death each week. I'm astounded at the large number of friends—some old, some young—currently battling cancer and other health issues. Aging brings a slew of aches and pains and hindrances to activity. Finances can disappear in a flash. As I write this, California has five major fires ravaging the countryside, with the Thomas fire in Ventura and Santa Barbara Counties alone consuming over a quarter of a million acres and leaving more than 1,000 burned buildings in its wake. More than 750 of those destroyed properties are family homes. Gone.

This shouldn't surprise us. Jesus promised, "Here on earth you will have many trials and sorrows" (John 16:33 NLT). We've all personally experienced that, and each of the faithful apostles (except John) were killed for their faith.

How do we respond? Often we puke and quit. A lot of bikers quit riding after their first spill. One media rider with the Thunderbirds couldn't take the physical pressures of the flight and ended it midway. In our faith, sometimes we continue following, but we don't extend ourselves; we stay in our comfort zone. We lose our edge, the joy of trusting and obeying God with no reservations. We miss a lot of joy and adventure that way. And successes.

Our option is to puke and rally. In part, expecting hard times will decrease our frustration a bit when they arrive. We aren't blindsided by them. That helps. It doesn't eliminate the pain and loss, but it helps. So expect some hard times. But we need more than anticipation. We need perseverance. Keeping on.

We don't give up that edge in our faith. We decide to carry on. We may refine our goals and hopes, but we keep them. We don't retreat.

Why should we rally? A lot of reasons. So we can stay in the game and gain the prize. So we can be used to touch people for Jesus. So we can use the pain to develop our faith, to grow in wisdom in handling setbacks. How do we accomplish this? There's a simple promise: "The one who is in you is greater than the one who is in the world" (1 John 4:4). We rely on God's presence for strength.

And we turn a loss into a victory. Sometimes the loss can be a necessary intermediate step to teach us. God can allow them to keep us from going in a direction that could damage us more.

And we will grow: "Consider it pure joy, my brothers and sisters, whenever you face trials of many kinds, because you know that the testing of your faith develops perseverance. Let perseverance finish its work so that you may be mature and complete, not lacking anything" (James 1:2-4). How do we become complete and mature spiritually? By rallying after we puke.

Ironic, isn't it? When the world hits us and we puke, we rely on Jesus' presence in us to not let the world win. That gives us more strength, and the next hit isn't as hard. So we turn the attacks into an ability to handle the next ones. And trust me, they will come.

For example, I've told you how Brad collided with a deer and broke several ribs, his collarbone, and scapula as well as a collapsed lung and needed to be airlifted to a hospital for treatment. Mick and I rode our bikes to the hospital. Brad's first comment was "How's the bike?" We assured him the minor damage could be fixed and he grinned and asked, "Next year, where we going?"

KICK-STARTING THE APPLICATION

What is your default when you encounter tough times? Has following Jesus altered that? If so, how? What has been your biggest difficulty in rallying from obstacles? How can you make progress in dealing with that? Think of a time when you rallied. What helped you get through it? How can you use that in the future?

42

CONSEQUENCES OF OVERCONFIDENCE

When Unguarded Strengths Become a Weakness

In honor of how relatively small events coupled with overconfidence can lead to problems, leading at least to embarrassment, I offer the following true confession. One June, the Gray Hogs pulled into Las Vegas when the temperature measured 109. We needed food and gas. In-N-Out took care of the former, Chevron the latter.

Our next stop, Cedar City, was 180 miles to the north, and another 130 would get us to Richfield, Utah, to meet the rest of our group. Since the tank on my ST1300 held 7.7 gallons and the bike easily averaged 45 mpg, I was confident I could go 350 miles, and we just had 310 to go. So I passed on gassing up in Cedar City.

I discovered my first miscalculation when I saw the distance signs as we were riding over the mountains to Highway 89. I read the map wrong regarding the distance from Cedar City as 89, and the 310 miles became 340. It was still in range, though, so I passed on the mom-and-pop station somewhere in Utah while the others gassed up. Yeah, I smirked. Okay, more than once.

We were cruising along the serene farmland bisected by the Sevier

River when I noticed my gas gauge drop more than I expected. Much more. The closer I came to Richfield, the more it dropped. So I slowed down. Then I slowed down some more, and Mick flew on ahead while Brad stayed with the slowpoke. When I crested the last hill before our exit, my motor died. Not even a cough to warn me. I pulled in the clutch, put the bike in neutral, and coasted the last half mile up to the pump. (Okay, I might have pushed it the last few feet.)

But when I filled the bone-dry tank, it only took 7.4 gallons. Second issue. Honda had proclaimed the capacity as 7.7. That night I reread the manual. It holds 7.7 gallons…when the bike is totally upright—not leaning. I reworked the math: 7.4 gallons at 45 mpg yields 333 miles. Pretty close. But not quite enough.

Ironically, the only bike to run out of gas on the trip was the one with the largest tank and the best mpg and the most confident driver. God has humorous methods to build our humility, doesn't he? But it suggests an important spiritual principle.

This wisdom from Oswald Chambers bears repeating: "An unguarded strength is a double weakness."[1] Mick's bike had the shortest range of all the Hogs. He brought an extra can of gas but never used it because he often stopped for a fresh tank. My overconfidence was born in the belief that my bike had the longest range of the Hogs, and yet I found myself falling short. I ended up pushing my bike to the gas pump. If I had tanked up just once during those two gas stops along the way, I would have been fine.

Isn't following Jesus like that a lot? For whatever reason, experience or just chance or our spiritual DNA, we think we have a decent amount of spiritual strength. Or maybe we just value obedience in an area quite strongly. So we don't guard it, and it turns and bites us in the butt. Growing up in church benefitted me with a solid value system. Some areas were definite—no shades of gray. And even when I wandered away from God, I maintained the importance of those two. Looking back now, I suspected I'd likely return at some point, so I wanted to keep those bases covered.

My first days after coming back to God brought a tremendous intimacy with him and a renewed commitment to live his life. He astounded me with his love and care and transforming power. Yet the two greatest sins of my life both occurred during a one-week period when I felt phenomenally close to him. With the benefit of hindsight, I thought if I could handle the temptations in those two issues when I wasn't walking with God, then with him they would be easier. I felt strong. I was overconfident. And I fell.

We expect Satan to focus on the areas of our weakness. And he does this effectively. Moses regularly struggled with his temper, Samson with sexual temptation, Peter with impulsiveness. And they all fell repeatedly in their areas of weakness. Thankfully, the classic verse on resisting temptation provides an escape hatch: "God is faithful; he will not let you be tempted beyond what you can bear. But when you are tempted, he will also provide a way out so that you can endure it" (1 Corinthians 10:13). We can handle temptation in our weak areas, one way or the other.

But sometimes the small openings work better for Satan. We feel confident. We've had success. We have a huge gas tank and good mileage, so we feel safe. But that strength becomes our greatest vulnerability when we don't guard it. That's why the apostle Paul cautioned us to "watch your life and doctrine closely. Persevere in them, because if you do, you will save both yourself and your hearers" (1 Timothy 4:16).

So I guess we have to pay attention to temptation in all arenas, right? If we do, we won't need to push our bike the last five feet to heaven.

KICK-STARTING THE APPLICATION

We often focus on strengthening our weaknesses and relying on our strengths. What are some of your key weaknesses that you need to pay regular attention to? Have they caused you trouble in the past? What helps you keep your guard up in these areas?

To flip the coin, what are some of your spiritual strengths, ones you have a decent handle on when resisting temptation? Have you ever fallen in these areas? What caused you to be vulnerable? In doing a temptation assessment, do you review these areas? Why or why not? How can you pay more attention to your strengths?

43

DRIVE DEFENSIVELY

Avoiding Disasters

For three years I commuted almost daily from Long Beach to Los Angeles, about 50 miles a day, roundtrip. I learned more about survival on SoCal freeways than I'd thought possible. Ironically, I felt safer splitting traffic lanes. I kept the bike between the cars when I would slide between them. I reasoned if they didn't see me, they'd at least see the other car, and I would have no problems.

But when I stayed supposedly safely in my own lane, drivers would look in my direction, often right into my eyes, and then pull over, forcing me to evade them. I'd honk and holler and on they came. A few times they came so close I kicked their door with my boot, but only if I had a clear getaway route.

My carnal desire for justice and self-preservation made me think about carrying a few steel balls in my jacket, large enough to fling at the homicidal car's window and break it. I resisted the temptation, but only barely. All of this reinforced some earlier advice given by a seasoned biker: Look on every car on the road as if the driver is intentionally out to get you. That's become automatic now more than 200,000 miles later. By the way, that approach works for driving four-wheeled vehicles as well.

But riding has changed in the nearly 50 years I've ridden, as have the dangers. A recent study, mentioned in chapter 23 from Virginia Tech, put five cameras on 100 bikes, with riders aged from 21 to 79, and covering over 360,000 miles. Riders experienced 30 crashes and 122 near crashes for a total of 152 events. Of the 99 events that involved another vehicle, 19 times a car hit the bike and 35 times a biker ran into the rear of another vehicle. The researchers concluded the two greatest risk factors were aggressive riding and inattention.

So we have to defend ourselves when we ride. We look out for cars that don't see us or don't care. We temper the aggressiveness of our riding, pay more attention, and look farther down the road than just right in front of us. That gives us the best chance of arriving safe and enjoying the journey. We also have those goals for navigating the spiritual life, so let's see how we can defend ourselves spiritually.

First, just as roads contain dangers to those on two wheels, life contains dangers to those on two legs. Too often we remain blissfully ignorant of the spiritual battle that rages around us unseen and often unsuspected.

When I was growing up, I heard about Murrieta Hot Springs Resort. So not long after Sheila and I moved to Temecula just next door, we wandered over to see it. A group called Alive Polarity then ran it, which we knew nothing about. Yet as we walked onto the property, I turned to Sheila and said, "Do you feel anything strange? Kind of like heavy dread?"

She sensed it too. Totally unexpected, and as a friend once said, we're not the kind of people who see demons behind every doorknob. So before we looked at much, we turned and exited. Once we were off the property that ill sense left. Later we learned of the cultic aspects of the group. A few years later Calvary Chapel purchased the property, and we went over to check it out. The sense was totally different.

Let's not go overboard, but realize life has spiritual dangers. "Stay alert! Watch out for your great enemy, the devil. He prowls around like a roaring lion, looking for someone to devour" (1 Peter 5:8 NLT). Satan is alive and active in our world. His goal—our destruction. Let's follow Peter's metaphor a bit more. Lions sometimes ambush their prey, waiting unseen until lunch strolls up. At other times they quietly stalk dinner and charge when they're within 100 feet. Often they swipe at an animal's hindquarters to knock it off balance.

Ever walk right into a temptation, totally unaware of the danger until it pounced? Ever get surprised at how fast a temptation arrives out of nowhere? Ever been knocked off balance spiritually by a relatively minor event, one that leaves you questioning and vulnerable?

The solution is to keep in mind that we live in a dangerous world where temptations abound. The joy that Satan offers comes with damage attached. He has no desire to do good to us. So we have to stay alert.

And analyze the spiritual implications of each event. Okay, not the brand of toothpaste, but you get the idea. The bike accident study suggested one of the best strategies to staying safe is to look ahead more. Looking down the spiritual road can minimize ambushes. Paul advised that as well: "Test everything... Hold on to what is good. Stay away from every kind of evil" (1 Thessalonians 5:21-22 NLT). *The Message* gives a nice slant on that first phrase: "Don't be gullible."

Gullible people believe what's on the surface. They listen to whatever someone else says, regardless of who they are. They believe everything they read on Facebook. They don't probe. They don't ask questions. They don't pray for God to let them sense the dangers. As a result, their chances of going down increase.

So we check it all out. We see what God's Word says about the issue. We remember how similar events from our past worked out. We get good advice from friends. We pray. And sometimes, instead of just jumping into some murky water, we stick a toe in first. We don't commit too soon. And if we find the water holds danger, we get out. Fast!

Do you remember Joseph's response when his boss's wife came on to him? He didn't cuddle, he didn't have a long conversation with why they shouldn't get involved. He got out of Dodge. Right away. And if you read the story in Genesis 39:7-20, he ended up being sent to prison when he was falsely accused of sexual assault. But better in a prison of stone than a prison of sin.

Sure, life is dangerous. But we can make it through. With a smile.

KICK-STARTING THE APPLICATION

How often do you deliberately think about the unseen spiritual reality? Think of a time you were oblivious and got ambushed. How could you have avoided it? What is one new approach you can take this week to live more carefully?

44

ADDICTIONS

When Having a Few Helps

My first and almost forced ride on a Honda Trail 90 interested me. Watching *Easy Rider* during finals week as a college senior entranced me. But buying a Honda 350 Scrambler and taking it to Canada hooked me. In the 49 years since then, I've ridden enough to build calluses on my rump, to get a lot of grease under my nails, and I'm lucky enough not to have developed carpal tunnel syndrome in my right wrist.

Call it a bike addiction and I won't argue. But I have more.

Addictions

Once
> *under two minutes*
> *I ate an entire berry pie*

Thereby
> *demonstrating my near addiction to berry pie*
> *proving my gluttony*
> *winning the blue ribbon*
> *losing my love for berries for years*

But today
> *having ridden the Honda sport touring bike almost 600 miles*

having seen the massiveness of your mountains
and the rolling green hills and verdant pastures
having smelled new-mown hay and rain-infused sage and
   mint
having viewed yearling deer grazing and red-tailed hawks
   soaring and chipmunks scurrying
having observed placid lakes and rushing rivers and slow
   irrigation ditches
my addiction to you
merely grows

Addictions plague our society. From substance abuse to sexual predators. From eating to exercise. From workaholism to couch potatoes. Too much of damaging actions or substances merely increases the devastation, but we can also hurt ourselves by too much of otherwise good things. Not long ago there was a news story about a woman who drank too much water and died because of that. Water is generally a pretty helpful requirement for staying alive. But not in this case.

Seems like some consider almost every problem qualifies as an addiction, but it exceeds that. Dictionary.com defines addiction as "being enslaved to a habit or practice or to something that is psychologically or physically habit-forming, as narcotics, to such an extent that its cessation causes severe trauma."

By much of that definition, I may have an addiction to God. To seeing his majesty and power and love expressed in his creation. To establishing regular practices that enhance my closeness with him. To wanting more of him. To needing regular fixes. Fixes of him and his creation that so well express his heart.

Two caveats here. Please don't think I'm minimizing the severe problems brought by addictions. They hurt our society significantly, and we all likely have friends and families or selves who have battled them and battle them still. The term *addiction* carries an exceptionally negative connotation because it damages people. But a healthy addiction to God doesn't damage us. Rather, it provides the road map to maximum life. So let's have a little fun and explore addiction to God based on that definition!

First, we do become slaves. Before Jesus, sin enslaved us and controlled our lives. But we've changed masters when we start to follow Jesus, and we give that role to God: "You have been set free from sin and have become slaves to God" (Romans 6:22). Or God becomes the most important priority in our lives. You have to admit there's at least some similarity, so let's check off the first box.

Second, knowing Jesus grows into a habit. Most of us start a bit slow. Maybe a friend is following Jesus. Possibly going to a home group or worship service. We get intrigued, become regular, and then finally decide to follow. We connect with some others. We read some Bible verses a pastor gave us, then we start to read a book in the Bible. Maybe a book on the Christian life. And we continue to go deeper. We hunger to know God's values and incorporate them more and more in our lives. We find a purpose that brings unity to our lives, one we arrange the various elements around. Check this box now.

Third, we experience trauma if we don't get our fix. On a recent road trip Sheila and I drove 450 miles all Saturday to Sedona, Arizona, and arrived wiped out. So sleeping in on Sunday morning came naturally. But when we arrived home the next Saturday, I made sure to hit the rack early because I deeply missed worshipping. Peter experienced something similar. Jesus said some hard things, and a bunch of people left. Discouraged, he asked the disciples if they wanted to leave as well. Peter came through: "Lord, to whom shall we go? You have the words of eternal life" (John 6:68). Once we genuinely connect with Jesus, we're lost without him. Another box checked.

The fourth trait contrasts with the tone of the definition, because this addiction benefits us. And the more we get, the more we want.

Let's look at all of an earlier verse: "You have been set free from sin and have become slaves to God, the *benefit you reap leads to holiness*, and the result is eternal life" (Romans 6:22). We get a continually changing life of living out God's values. Our character changes and our consciences don't bug us as much. We get an abundant life now and have confidence that death doesn't end us; we get heaven after. Not a bad addiction.

KICK-STARTING THE APPLICATION

Based on the above, has God addicted you? Are you an abstainer or a casual user? Why did you answer like that? Should you be where you are? What keeps you there? Try to think of one area that lessens your closeness with God. Why is that important to you? Does that area have the chance of continuing after your earthly life ends? Most significantly, is Jesus the Lord and boss of your life? If you've not made that commitment, does anything keep you from making it now?

45

DIFFERENT STROKES

Different Folks

One September the Gray Hogs rode from the Northwest, south through Washington, pretty much all the way down the Oregon coast, and all the way down the California coast, hitting the coastal redwoods, Big Sur, Highway 101, and a lot more. Yeah, we caught some rain with the beautiful country. But looking back, what most struck me was how different the three of us were. Start with the bikes.

Jerry rides a Honda Gold Wing, the ultimate touring bike. The powerful six-cylinder motor can fly, but it's so smooth the best metaphor is a nice recliner.

Mick rode a Wing as well for years until he thought he was done riding and gave it to his son-in-law. Several months later, when his wife kindly pointed out, "This man is not finished riding," he bought a Honda Shadow, a cool town-cruising V-twin, and continued with our road trips. His bike looks the most like a classic ride, but its low gearing makes climbing mountains an exercise in patience. (For all of us.)

I have a red Honda ST1300, a fine blend of touring and town riding.

That September ride was 3,000 miles long, and it was handled nicely by all three very different bikes.

I guess that's appropriate, that the bike differences match the biker differences. Whenever we hit a town, Mick looks for a Dairy Queen to grab a Blizzard. Of course, I'm forced to go along and get one—usually a chocolate-chip cookie dough. Jerry searches for a movie theater and then tries to convince the rest of us to join him. We have at times, but he's also abandoned us for several hours to catch the latest. I want to find a museum or a brew pub. Sometimes they'll join me, but I've been known to abandon them a few times. Like Jerry.

But we've ridden together for decades. We're the core of a group that's hung in there a long time. Probably a dozen others have cycled through on a ride or two, but the three of us remain. Well, Brad's been a part for the last few years, although he missed this trip—so our core is really four. Why and what does that mean for spiritual formation?

The four of us share three common denominators. First, we all love God and try to craft our lives to follow him. We've all known him for decades and have made solid commitments. Second, we all love bikes and long cross-country tours. Yeah, we ride different scooters, but we enjoy riding in similar country. Third, we've built a long history based on what we share, not how we differ. I've known Jerry since high school. Mick shortly after. And although Brad is fairly new, he's Mick's nephew. So we all share a history. Yes, we frustrate each other at times. Yes, the voices sometimes get a bit sharp. Yes, we have different ideas about the best route to a destination. Yes, we have different preferences about how fast we should roam the roadways.

But as long as we can ride and for as long as God wills, the Gray Hogs will stick together.

Now here's the spiritual link. At the start of this September trip, I spent several days with my sister and her husband in Redding and attended their small group, one that is active, larger than the experts say is optimal, ministers to one another, and has stuck together for years. When they asked themselves why, this outsider observer chimed in. They share a love of God, have common interests, and have built a history together. Those elements yield a strength that overpowers differences. A lot like the Gray Hogs.

Deep and continuing connections with others form a vital part of following Jesus, serving others, and being served when needed. Ponder how you can incorporate the following four goals in your life to better connect.

First, build a genuine love for God and his people and express it. Jesus stressed the last: "Your love for one another will prove to the world that you are my disciples" (John 13:35 NLT). If love doesn't act, it really isn't love. Love gives, so give. Love serves, so serve.

Second, work stuff out. All followers still have a sin nature, so we'll grate on each other. Some friction can be ignored, but if it begins to impact our relationships or lingers in our mind, then we do best to address it. Let's smooth things out. "If it is possible, as far as it depends on you, live at peace with everyone" (Romans 12:18). Not all relationships can be repaired, and sometimes we just don't fit or connect with others. Several good guys rode with us a time or two, but sometimes the fit just wasn't there. But let's do our best.

Third, embrace differences—like the Hogs, with different bikes and different riding styles and different preferences. Mick has found some roads I wouldn't have tried. Jerry has gotten great deals on hotel rooms I wouldn't have found. Brad blesses us with his easygoing nature. I like that. "Just as each of us has one body with many members, and these members do not all have the same function, so in Christ we, though many, form one body, and each member belongs to all the others" (Romans 12:4-5).

Fourth, laugh at the hardships. The Hogs have been caught in downpours where our bikes hydroplaned, Brad T-boned a deer and needed to be life-flighted, and our other misadventures could fill a book. Wait, they kind of do that, right? But we can obsess on the problems or choose to pull some good from them. "Consider it pure joy, my brothers and sisters, whenever you face trials of many kinds" (James 1:2). Honestly, that's not always easy, but it usually works. And sometimes the laughter can only come a bit after.

KICK-STARTING THE APPLICATION

How involved are you with others on a regular, deep, committed basis? Have you seen the effect of that in your intimacy with God? What and why? Do you get a sense to craft more connections with fellow Christians? A local church? Regardless of your current level, how can you enhance that? Look at those three elements that connect the Gray Hogs and my sister's small group. How well do you do in them?

46

HARD TIMES

Keeping Disappointment from Flowing into Frustration

Several years back, my blog post on *Unconventional* featured a serene pic of two nice-looking bikes in the California redwoods on an early September morning. Try to imagine the shadows, a light fog about 20 feet high, and the majestic redwoods. But the surface serenity never yields a clue to the hard times those bikes and another experienced on that trip. Nor the experiences of their riders. The red Honda ST1300 sports a new front tire with only 100 miles on it. The fork seals had been replaced improperly just before the trip. One side of the tire wore more than the other, and I struggled to find a mechanic who could replace the half-bald tire, desperately searching the Oregon and California coasts until we reached Fort Bragg.

The exceptionally clean charcoal Gold Wing never reveals the problems Jerry had when his cruise control became intermittent and left him with a cramp in his right arm. Yeah, we heard a lot about that from him.

Mick's blue Honda Shadow 1100 isn't in this picture, but he had a range of only 130 miles, so one saddlebag carried a gallon can of gas— just in case. And when we hit an incline, his city street gearing made the climb an exercise in patience. Or his bike was slow. Very slow.

Mick also had to haul a CPAP machine around so he wouldn't suddenly stop breathing while he slept at night.

Body wise, Jerry's bad back forced him to pack a special chair he would sleep in at motel rooms. And you know we razzed him about that. (A lot!)

I tweaked my back the week before, when I helped move a gazebo. While I was fine when I was riding, I woke up each morning with a sore back.

But (and the important information always comes after the but) none of us are about to quit riding. We are already planning next year's ride. A lot of bikers quit, though. Some start off riding and ride less and less until they quit. Or they tire of it and quit. Or they fear getting hurt and they quit. The Hogs have faced all these, and we still ride. The joy and peace and oneness with nature and our relationships overpowers our fears and difficulties. And we don't expect blue skies all the time.

We all face disappointments. They can come from our families, our relationships, our health, our finances, our jobs, our neighbors...well, any aspect of life. And since stuff flows downhill, we need to keep unmet expectations from becoming frustrations. Let's explore how.

Decades ago, a speaker explained how frustration lives in the land between expectations and reality. Unrealistic expectations increase our frustrations. So we can decrease frustration by carefully controlling what we expect. There's one major qualification: hopes don't rise to the level of expectation. I hope for a lot of things, like winning the Publishers Clearing House sweepstakes, but I don't expect it to ever happen, so I don't get frustrated when I don't win. Yeah, someone has to win, but the odds are greatly against this someone being anyone in particular. I hope some reader might gift me with a brand-new custom-outfitted ST1300. But...

So we expect hard times to be a normal part of life. We expect our hopes may never become realities. Not that we become pessimists, just hopeful realists. Jesus promised as much: "I have told you all this so that you may have peace in me. Here on earth you will have many trials and sorrows. But take heart, because I have overcome the world" (John 16:33 NLT). Bikes break down. Deer collide with us. People wear on us. Rain pummels us. But we ride, not expecting continual blue skies. We hope for them, but we don't expect them.

When trials arrive, we acknowledge them. Health generally doesn't associate with hiding from reality. So we try to identify the source if we can. We may have caused it, so we acknowledge that and move on. Sometimes another person brought it to us through nothing we did. If so, we try to resolve it as best we can. When we can't, we forgive and move on. It may be without them, but we move on. When the hard times came randomly, we quietly whisper, "Life sucks sometimes," and move on.

And most important, we lean on God. Frankly, leaning on God sometimes makes no more sense to our finite minds than does leaning a bike into a curve at speed. But that lean allows us to get through the curve. And reminding ourselves that God loves us in all of our trials and failures, that he always works for good, allows us to survive the curves of life.

This verse works well with the previous one: "The one who is in you is greater than the one who is in the world" (1 John 4:4). We're promised troubles, so we need to avoid unrealistic blue-sky expectations. But Jesus, the one in us, transcends the power of the world to bring us down.

We ride. We get hammered with rain and troubles. But we go with Jesus and do fine.

KICK-STARTING THE APPLICATION

Have you faced frustrations that come from unrealized expectations? What were some specific events? Ponder why they came and brought frustration. What were your expectations before the event? What troubles are you facing now? What influence do they have on your closeness to God? Do you expect the Christian life to be easy? Why does this cause disappointment? Try to list at list six benefits that you have from following Jesus when frustrations come. Review these.

47

LET A BIKE BE A BIKE

Becoming the Genuine You

With a roar of motors, we pulled out of the church at 8 a.m. Our destination was Julian, an Old West mining town in San Diego County. The first and prime part of the ride was the South Grade Road on Palomar Mountain. Some experts claim this and the Tail of the Dragon at Deal's Gap in Tennessee lay title to the most twisty, difficult biker roads in America.

We stopped at the base to preview the next seven miles, to be celebrated with breakfast or pie at Mother's Kitchen at the top. With a sport bike, a sport touring bike, and three Harley cruisers, our pace was varied, but I wanted to keep us all fairly close. So I took it slow with my sport tourer, and Ben was right behind me on his sport bike. He could have blown my doors off, metaphorically. Ruben, John, and Scott followed pretty close on their cruisers.

After a few miles of taking it easy, my bike almost begged out loud to move. Faster. So I gradually kicked up my speed. Ben stayed close, but a gap widened with the cruisers. They soon dropped out of sight as Ben and I let our bikes play the curves, accelerating, braking, leaning, and using our handlebars to maximize our speed. No, we didn't get crazy out of control, but our grins were pretty wide, and we had to wait a bit for the others at the top. Quite a bit.

When they arrived, Ruben, smiling, said, "I thought you were gonna stay close."

I responded, "I had to let the bike be a bike." My bike was designed to go quicker up the curvy road than a car or even most large cruising bikes. That was its purpose, its teleology.

Ruben quipped, "So our bikes don't have the same purpose to go fast?"

We had a nicely spirited discussion about how various styles of bikes are designed for different types of riding. Sport bikes go fast and handle the turns, so they lean nicely into the curves. Cruisers are built for speed, but they ride best in a fairly straight line with remarkable stability. Sport tourers have more stability than sport bikes and corner nicely, but they aren't as quick. Kind of in between the two.

That discussion prompted this chapter. We need to identify and develop and exercise our unique design, which will maximize our personal Christlikeness. Why is this crucial? At all ages, we feel the pressure to conform. Paul recognized it: "Don't let the world around you squeeze you into its own mould, but let God re-mould your minds from within, so that you may prove in practice that the plan of God for you is good...and moves toward the goal of true maturity" (Romans 12:2 PHILLIPS).

We want to fit in. To be like others. And the world wants us to do that. Frankly, if we don't fit in some, we become separated from significant interactions with others. A hermit. And in so doing we lose all chances to impact our world.

But if we carve away pieces of ourselves to match what others expect, we find nothing is left of us. Just a copy of others. Sport bikes don't cruise like Harleys. Harleys don't corner like sport bikes. They each need to follow their design and purpose. Like us.

God created us all with unique abilities and interests and experiences, which allow us to have an impact no other individual can give.

We shouldn't all be pastors, but some should. We shouldn't all be building contractors, but some should. We, well, you get the point. In 1 Corinthians 12, Paul compares the church, the body of Christ, to a physical body. If all parts were a foot, we couldn't experience the joy of coffee. But in our differences, we work together for the greater good.

So let's examine five steps to ponder on your next ride to better craft your life to find and be the best you.

1. Know your human self. Identify your strengths, weak areas, interests, joys, personality. Pray about this and get input from wise friends who can be impartial. They often have more perspective than we do about ourselves. Think about some key life experiences that have helped to shape you.

2. Know your spiritual self, as you can be in God. Look ahead. How can you develop and grow and serve? What spiritual gifts and heart and successes and failures can guide you to becoming the ideal you?

3. Be true to numbers 1 and 2 above. As God directs, craft your life to be the genuine you. Make deliberate decisions to develop in that direction by including these two in your choices. Don't ignore them.

4. Minimize doing what doesn't match numbers 1 and 2 above. Discover which options merely distract you from the best. And realize that we have to pay a lot of dues in life to get by, so don't think you can avoid them all. Paying dues allows us to move from spiritual apprentice to the journeyman level.

5. Trust in God to guide and empower you in the process. Don't try to do it all on your own, but rely on his strength and love.

And as you do this, you'll get to the top of your mountain in the manner that matches who you are. Whether blasting up on a fast, nimble sport bike or leisurely cruising on a V-Twin or splitting the difference on a sport touring bike, let your bike be its kind of bike.

KICK-STARTING THE APPLICATION

Have you felt pressure from others or society to fit in to their expectations? How much did you conform to their desires? Have you spent very much time examining who you are? If not, why not? If so, what have you found? What observations have others made about your abilities and traits and gifts? How does the direction of your life match the purpose God has for you? What change can you make this week to be the you God designed you to be?

48

GET IN THE WORLD

Engage with the World...Both of Them

Our biker crew recently rode through Las Vegas on I-15 with the temperature a bit above 100, and I enjoyed the warmth in a strange way. A dry heat, right? I tried to remember that a few days later when we pulled out of Alpine, Wyoming, with the temperature at 30, but it soon dropped to 28 and stayed like that for an hour. In a strange manner, I embraced that too. Later we drove past some alfalfa fields, many newly mown, and the scent reminded me of the hay barn at our old family farm.

Half a mile before we saw the truck, I knew it was hauling onions from the faint aroma that we rode through. When the rain hit, even as I huddled behind my windshield, I enjoyed the cleansing. The eagle soaring above us in Yellowstone could only have been seen on a bike (well, a convertible would have worked too). And the sense of closeness to and danger from a magnificent buffalo, walking just four feet away and down the center of the road would never have been the same in a car.

I ride to engage with the world. Bikes don't provide a safe steel cage that insulates you from God's creation. Cars do. Bikes only provide protection by maneuverability and power to get out of dicey situations, which often isn't enough. Cars provide much more. But when

I can choose, I choose a bike. Even around town a lot. Experiencing the world that God so graciously gave us seems worth the risk. God got it right when he pronounced six times that the world he had just created was good (Genesis 1). Enjoying and appreciating his creation is worship.

Not everyone likes giving up safety and comfort to better connect with the natural world, and I get it. Some love to live inside, comfortable and warm, and they most enjoy beautiful nature scenes through a window. Body thermostats, physical abilities, and a lot more contribute, and I understand this even as I desire to experience nature more directly.

But riding a motorcycle in the physical world provides a metaphor for engagement in the people world. Something even more important than enjoying nature. As followers of Jesus, the biker metaphor encourages all of us to be in the social world, to engage with it. Not to hide from it. Yes, that has risks, but it's our call as Christians. Jesus taught us as much: "My prayer is not that you take them out of the world but that you protect them from the evil one. They are not of the world, even as I am not of it" (John 17:15-16). We often paraphrase that as "we're in the world but not of it," and that nicely expresses the balance.

So how do we engage with the world yet not be corrupted by it? Let's examine four principles.

First, we live in the world but shouldn't let it determine our values. God does that. We followers miss that in many ways. Some of us are so into identifying with the world that we become just like them, and we lose any chance of impacting them for God. Some of us withdraw from what we don't agree with, and we lose any chance of impacting them for God. So we miss our mission. The apostle Paul warned us: "Don't let the world around you squeeze you into its own mould, but let God re-mould your minds from within" (Romans 12:2 PHILLIPS).

Second, view the people of the world with love—a love that chooses to act in their benefit regardless of their values, behaviors, politics, or likability. I appreciate the old cliché, "People won't care what you know [about Jesus] unless they know you care." We connect with humility, not a condescending or judgmental attitude that merely repels them. We don't have to agree, just be agreeable. The difference between the two is huge.

Third, engage with people. Spend time with unbelievers and intentionally build connections. Know the culture. Paul often quoted poets and philosophers. For us who ride, get to know the good qualities of bikes other than your ride. Again, don't accept the values, just know them and have the ability to converse about them. Does that suggest I need to build a little more familiarity with popular music, like rap? Hmm.

Fourth, our intimacy with Jesus directly links to our commitment to the mission he's given us: to tell about Jesus and the privilege we have of personally knowing the Creator of the universe. Let this be a foundation for the first three steps. Be intentional. Don't browbeat others or look down on them. Sometimes we need to craft a good relationship before we ever say a word, so let them see a follower of Jesus as an engaging person who cares. I love the line often attributed to Francis of Assisi: "Preach the gospel at all times. When necessary, use words." While he likely didn't say this, it matches what he said, that our deeds should match our words.

As riders, we tend to love engaging with the natural world. As followers of Jesus, we need to love engaging with the social world.

KICK-STARTING THE APPLICATION

On that continuum of being in or withdrawn from the culture, where do you fit? Would that thrill Jesus? Ponder some ways you could get more personally connected with the society around you. On the continuum of being like the world in your values and behaviors or choosing your values and actions from God, where do you fit? Would that thrill Jesus? Ponder some ways you can preserve a biblical value system even as you interact with the world.

Last, identify one thing you can do this week to increase your interaction with the world in a godly manner.

49

LETTING DREAMS DIE

Addition by Subtraction

From our first discussions about the trip, I knew my memories would overwhelm me. Rich and I grew up in the same Long Beach church, but he long ago moved to South Dakota. Now we wanted to meet somewhere and ride to SoCal. So we made plans to meet halfway, in Taos, New Mexico, and find some new back roads. But the Taos area held no new roads for me.

About 40 years ago a mission group asked me and a friend to lead a mission trip to Penasco, about 25 miles outside Taos. I repeated that the next year, and Taos enticed me to live there. It may not have been heaven, but it was next door.

The area is full of high mountains and valleys—Penasco was just under 8,000 feet, and Taos, at 7,000, marked the beginning of the mountains that climbed to over 13,000 feet. The friendly and hospitable people are a blend of Pueblo Indian and Hispanic and Anglo. Food like I'd never tasted. Sopapillas and stacked enchiladas and bowls of green chili. Beautiful trout streams. They seemed like my personal fisheries.

I lived in a log cabin at 8,500 feet, more than three miles off the nearest asphalt, surrounded by national forest. Used a road grader to plow the snow. Skied the driest powder I could imagine, often with no tracks to follow. Historical—the nearby pueblo has been occupied for about a thousand years, and the town of Taos was established in 1615. Before Plymouth. And premier bike country. I'd come home to a place I'd never been before.

At first, my memories were held at bay for the first solo part of the ride from Temecula, but they flooded back and forced me to stop after turning off Highway 68 onto Highway 75 on the road to Penasco. I felt home again. Why did I ever leave paradise?

You see, 40 years before I'd loudly proclaimed I'd never move back to SoCal. Adamantly. I suspect you know how God reacts to such plans. After two years I realized that my time in Taos, while a dream, wasn't a destination. God sent me there so the First Baptist Church could love me back into the ministry. So I told my wife that night, on our daily call, that I really missed Taos, but I didn't regret leaving. Why?

God will bring many things into our lives for a season. To prepare us. To wait for the right time. To prepare others for us. To grace us with good memories. My mom had a funny line about that. She knew it didn't match the Bible's meaning, but it held truth. When something bad occurred, she'd smile and quote part of Matthew 7:28: "It came to pass, it didn't come to stay." I found that phrase used 66 times in the King James Version. Taos, for me, came to pass, not to stay.

One afternoon God clearly told me to leave. For ministry. So I left.

How do we respond when good things, when dreams, pass? And they will. They touch us for a season, but seasons end. Here are three tips.

First, cling to God, not things or places or stuff. Our faith reaches maturity and brings comfort when we value knowing and having Jesus above all else.

> If you decide for God, living a life of God-worship, it fol-
> lows that you don't fuss about what's on the table at meal-
> times or whether the clothes in your closet are in fashion.
> There is far more to your life than the food you put in your
> stomach, more to your outer appearance than the clothes
> you hang on your body…Steep your life in God-reality,
> God-initiative, God-provisions. Don't worry about miss-
> ing out. You'll find all your everyday human concerns will
> be met (Matthew 6:25,33 MSG).

Keep a loose grip on the stuff of the material world and a tight grip on God.

Second, realize that many spots in life are way stations, not destinations. I thought accepting a call to pastor a church in Fallbrook fit the latter, but God revealed it as the former. Was that a mistake? Not at all. Our daughter met a local Fallbrook guy, and we have two awesome grandkids we would never have enjoyed otherwise. And being in Fallbrook led to planting a church in nearby Temecula, the most rewarding ministry of my career, and where we still live.

Keep in mind we can't always distinguish early on between way stations and destinations, so keep your grip loose. Enjoy it, cherish it, but don't assume permanency.

Third, realize that leaving a dream doesn't mean giving it up, just moving up. My satisfying life now wouldn't exist without my time in Taos. I wouldn't have entered the ministry. Wouldn't have met the lady who became my wife. Her daughter wouldn't have met her husband. Wouldn't have experienced two marvelous grandchildren. Wouldn't have written any books.

But I knew none of that when God said, "Go." Like Abram, I went. To obey him. Somewhat blindly, to be frank.

I *really* miss Taos, sopapillas, and the people and the land. I thank God I experienced them. But I let that dream go for something better.

Serving him. And in that serving, he blessed me in ways greater than Taos. Yes, I miss Taos, but I made a move up. God is good.

KICK-STARTING THE APPLICATION

Do you have a dream life? Do you live it or are you still dreaming? Is there something in your life right now, something that is good and godly and enjoyable, that if you let it go, might allow God to do something greater? Do you get a sense of that? Are you willing to ask God about it? What most holds you back? Could it be time to release your Taos?

50

FRESH ADVENTURES

Familiarity Empowers New Approaches

One early June morning at 4:30, I pulled the Honda ST1300 out of its comfortable garage for a Gray Hogs ride with our ever-present goal of finding fresh asphalt. We've covered a lot of territory and roads, so new brings smiles to our faces. The upcoming trip hit five states (California, Nevada, Oregon, Washington, and Idaho) and a foreign country (Canada) and covered 3,800 miles in nine days. We retraced some familiar roads, but we discovered a lot of previously unridden routes, took the bikes on a free ferry ride across Kootenay Lake in Canada, and dodged a lot of drenching storms that forced us to continually redraw our plans.

Along with the new roads came a lot of new names, such as Ymir, Metalline, Sedro Wooley, Sultan, Skykomish, and Oronda. Exotic. A fresh adventure. But the prevalence of very familiar names struck me in this new country.

In the Antelope Valley, within the first hundred miles, I saw a sign for Joshua Street, reminding me of my grandson. In Redding, Palo Verde Avenue appeared, a bit confusing since I grew up on Palo Verde Avenue in Long Beach. Close by was Conant, the cross street just north of my Palo Verde. We rode through Long Beach, Washington.

I found a Westlake Avenue; I'd taught school in Westlake Village, California. Carson City, Nevada, had a Christensen Auto Repair, matching the last name of one of our crew. And if you knew Jerry, the idea of him with a wrench and working on a car would have you rolling on the floor.

Sweet ironies, finding so many reminders of my past in the midst of this new territory. And a fine metaphor for traveling with Jesus through life.

Historians say the only constant is change, and from a merely human perspective, I tend to agree. Life situations change. Jobs change. Technology changes. Our finances change. Relationships change. Our kids change. Churches and their leaders change. Styles of worship change. This morning before I began to write, the music festival Coachella released its upcoming line up of acts. A writer wondered whatever happened to rock. Hip-hop and rap dominated the playbill.

And, yes, change can increase stress. We lose much of the familiar. The unknown future can cause us to tremble a bit. But change in life comes despite our efforts.

The spiritual life also changes constantly—and it should. We learn more about the Bible. We grow closer to God. We get hammered by life events and our faith weakens or strengthens. Different people enter our lives and impact us. How we serve God can change. We learn from our experiences. I love looking back at the early years, just after returning to a dynamic relationship with Jesus. They had a special freshness and God moved. Yet I had some major flaws that needed decades to work out. So we rejoice in some parts of spiritual change, such as "our salvation is nearer now than when we first believed" (Romans 13:11). We get closer to wholeness all the time, and that's change.

We're on the spiritual road but not there yet, with much fresh ground to cover. Yet I've found God takes us (and me) in completely unanticipated directions. Some seem accidental, a few clearly come from him, others I fight against at the time. But God knows his stuff. Change.

So how do we navigate fresh spiritual asphalt on a road we've never encountered?

First, seek out the new. Embrace the changes that come uninvited. Don't expect life to remain constant, and that will ease some of the discomfort that change can bring. View walking with Jesus as an adventure into new territory. Don't get stuck in the rut that is just a grave where the ends haven't yet been filled in.

Second, take the familiar along. Too much new can be overwhelming, so balance it with the familiar, much like the familiar place names gave me a sense of place as I ventured into fresh places. That can balance us if we choose to view them as a foundation rather than an anchor. So what do we carry on the journey?

Most important, take the reality of God's presence with you. Remember, "the LORD your God will be with you wherever you go" (Joshua 1:9). His character will help us make good value decisions. His power will enable us to carry them out. His love will bring the comfort of his presence as we encounter what we never have before. And practice his presence. We know he's with us, but I need to regularly remind myself of that.

Take friends along on your journey. Good ones. Longtime ones. Newer ones. The companionship and help that friends have given me on bike trips parallels their roles in my life spiritually. Good friends speak truth into our lives, even when that's difficult. They give us the security to try new endeavors. They pick us up.

Take good memories and weave them into the new ones. Our memories remind us of what God has done before, and they give us courage as we embark on fresh adventures. Thinking of his prior acts leads us into the future. Part of this includes remembering the lessons we've learned. When I rode a chain-drive bike, I learned to check the tension each day. Why? Because I missed it one day, and the chain slipped off the sprocket and jammed the rear wheel.

The Christian life continually takes us on new and unanticipated roads. But the familiar gives a foundation in the change. Embrace it.

KICK-STARTING THE APPLICATION

Look back at some changes that you dreaded yet they worked out well. What did you learn from the process? When you rode some fresh spiritual asphalt, what best helped you navigate it? What most hurt? Do you see a fresh road coming up? How are you approaching it? What familiar aspects can you take along to help?

NOTES

Chapter 4: Risky Business

1. C.S. Lewis, *God in the Dock.*

Chapter 15: Getting Clean

1. https://www.merriam-webster.com/dictionary/stress.
2. "Research Findings on the Relationship Between Motorcycle Riding and Brain Stimulation," March 4, 2009, https://global.yamaha-motor.com/news/2009/0304/research.html.

Chapter 19: Go Along

1. Barna, "The State of the Church 2016," September 15, 2016, https://www.barna.com/research/state-church-2016/.

Chapter 23: Be a Boy Scout

1. Lance Oliver, "What Virginia Tech learned about how and why we crash our motorcycles," November 21, 2016, https://www.revzilla.com/common-tread/what-virginia-tech-learned-about-how-and-why-we-crash-our-motorcycles.
2. Oswald Chambers, *My Utmost for His Highest,* "April 19."

Chapter 37: Road Maps

1. https://science.nasa.gov/astrophysics/focus-areas/what-is-dark-energy.

Chapter 42: Consequences of Overconfidence

1. Oswald Chambers, *My Utmost for His Highest,* "April 19."

A NOTE FROM THE AUTHOR

I hope *God, a Motorcycle, and the Open Road* challenged you—to ride more, to love God more, to serve more, to grow more. This book gives a great metaphor about our journey with Jesus—how he can be seen in everyday events.

So let's keep this going, I love to connect with my readers. My blog, *Unconventional*, at timriter.com, has a fresh post each week about weaving faith into the fabric of our lives.

Also, I would love to do a sequel, with half the stories coming from you, fellow riders. If you have a story to tell, just shoot me an email at timriter@aol.com and we'll take it from there.

I do some speaking, having spent several decades as a pastor and university professor of communication, so if you need someone for a conference, message, or whatever, just get in touch with me at the email address just above.

Now, let's close as we began, with Psalm 45:3-4, "Ride majestically! Ride triumphantly! Ride on the side of truth! Ride for the righteous meek!" (MSG). And, ride safe!

BIBLE PERMISSIONS